IMAGES
of America

Around
SUSQUEHANNA
STATE PARK

This present-day map shows Susquehanna State Park, located in the northeastern section of Harford County, Maryland. The eastern boundary of the park is the shoreline of the Susquehanna River. To the north lies the village of Darlington, to the west the community of Churchville, and to the south, the city of Havre de Grace. Interstate 95 provides convenient access to the park from exit 89 (Havre de Grace).

IMAGES
of America

Around

SUSQUEHANNA
STATE PARK

Linda Noll

Published by Arcadia Publishing
Charleston SC, Chicago IL, Portsmouth NH, San Francisco CA

Printed in Great Britain

Library of Congress Catalog Card Number: 2005922060

For all general information contact Arcadia Publishing at:
Telephone 843-853-2070
Fax 843-853-0044
E-mail sales@arcadiapublishing.com
For customer service and orders:
Toll-Free 1-888-313-2665

Visit us on the internet at http://www.arcadiapublishing.com

VIEW OF THE SUSQUEHANNA RIVER. Capt. John Smith drew a map of the area's shoreline and inlets as he journeyed up the bay. He wrote in his diary, "Heaven and earth seem never to have agreed better to frame a place for man's commodius and delightful habitation." He named the Susquehanna River for himself as "Smith's Falles." His diary and map of the upper Chesapeake Bay country provides the first recorded information of the headwaters of Maryland's beautiful waterway. (Courtesy of David Duchon.)

CONTENTS

ACKNOWLEDGMENTS

I would like to thank everyone who has been involved with the writing of this book. I sincerely appreciate all of the interviews, phone calls, emails, and time spent in answering all of my questions and providing all the wonderful photographs.

Thanks to those who assisted with collecting the photographs for this book, especially Richard Sherrill, head of archives of the Historical Society of Harford County, for endless hours of "pulling" photographs for me and for sharing his unlimited knowledge of the Lapidum area. Thanks also to Dottie Meyer, volunteer at the society; Maryanna Skowronski, administrator; and Richard Herbig, president, for their support of this project. Thanks to Doug Washburn for his expertise in scanning these photos and to Mike Brunson at Ritz Camera for his professional scanning assistance. Thank you to Bill Bates, author, for his words of advice during this process. He has "been there, done that!"

I also owe thanks for the wonderful interview granted to me by Mary Macklem Peal soon after her 100th birthday in 2004, and to her daughter Mary and son-in-law Nelson Slye for sharing their family history with me through numerous emails and for providing family photographs for this book. My sincere appreciation goes also to those people who shared memories and photographs of the Level-Webster area with me: Nelson Bowman for his oral histories of life in the area, Elma Bowman, Isabelle Stearn, Robert Janssen, and Rebecca and Scott Walker. Thanks to Jo and Bernie Bodt and Pat and Art Elsner for sharing their knowledge of the canning industry in Harford County. And thanks to Gary Haslam, manager of Rocks-Susquehanna State Parks, for sharing information.

Thanks to my family for their understanding and encouragement throughout this writing project, and for not making too many demands on me: my husband, Richard; my children, Danielle, Michelle, Lynn, and Will, and grandson, Aidan; my parents, Catherine and Henry Peden Sr.; sons-in-law, Mark and Steve; and friend of the family, Bill Felter. This book is dedicated to them.

Thanks to the many volunteers at Steppingstone Museum for preserving our history, and making my job such a rewarding experience. Finally, thanks to my editor, Lauren Bobier, for her patience and guidance during the writing of this book.

INTRODUCTION

In 1773, by act of legislature, the Susquehanna River was designated the boundary between Harford and Cecil Counties. The mid-river boundary was chosen to avoid future controversies in regard to ferries, bridges, and fishing rights on this waterway. The Susquehanna, whose name means "smooth flowing stream," had a marked influence on the industrial and economic life of the territory. Historian C. Milton Wright, in his book *Harford Heritage*, stated elegantly:

> The wooded hills that form its watershed and the rippling waters that flow over the rocky boulders of its bed are scenes of rustic beauty that have been enjoyed by generations through the years. But the Susquehanna has not been solely for the natural beauty of its rocks and quiet coves or the stately grandeur of its nearby hills. From the time the earliest inhabitants settled on its rocky slopes, it has furnished valuable resources for those who dwelt in the forest and in the village through which it passed.

The Susquehanna River region was a place of settlement for the Susquehannock Indian tribes and for those pioneers brave enough to penetrate the wooded areas on its rocky shores. It furnished a waterway for transportation, and towns and villages sprang up along its banks. The villages of Stafford, Rock Run, and Lapidum boasted thriving industries with their gristmills, flint mills, iron forges, fish smokehouses, and icehouses. For over a century, the river made possible the canal that carried coal, grain, and lumber to the riverside communities. The deep water near its mouth became a commercial fishing ground for herring and shad and was the scene of a thriving industry until the early 20th century.

These river towns exist no more; however, the remnants of that way of life still linger, kept alive by descendents of those families who have lived in the area for many generations. Today this area and the historic structures still standing are preserved by the Maryland State Department of Natural Resources in Susquehanna State Park. The park's Steppingstone Museum preserves the rural arts and crafts of the region through its exhibits of thousands of artifacts donated by many of those descendants. The museum provides a historical journey for those who decide to wander off the beaten path and take a step back in time.

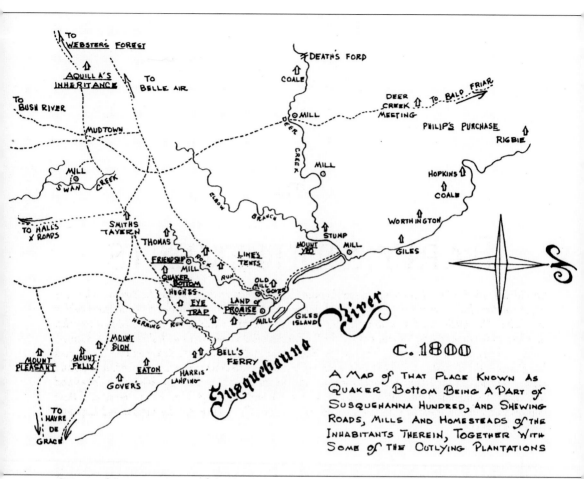

MAP, C. 1800. This map shows the region around the Susquehanna River which is today part of the state park. The map legend reads "A map of that place known as Quaker Bottom being a part of Susquehanna Hundred, and shewing roads, mills and homesteads of the inhabitants therein, together with some of the outlying plantations." (Courtesy of Steppingstone Museum Archives.)

One

EARLY SETTLEMENTS

On July 24, 1608, Capt. John Smith of the Virginia Colony sailed up the Chesapeake Bay to explore the upper country. It was on this voyage that Smith encountered a tribe of hunting Native Americans calling themselves "Susquehannocks" who were also fierce warriors and rivals of the nearby Massawomeks. Smith recorded in his diary, "About sixty of the Sasquesahonocks came to us with skins, bowes, arrows, beads, swords, and tobacco pipes for presents. Such great and well proportioned men for they seemed like giants to the English. . . . These are the strangest people of all these countries, both in language and attire." The fate of the Susquehannocks was decided by their continued warfare with other tribes and by disease. By the late 17th century, land grants were awarded to English colonists who named their villages in the manner of their previous occupants, such as Conowingo (at the rapids) and Lapidum (place of rocks).

WOODED SCENE. Most of the beautiful woodlands of the Susquehanna State Park remain virtually undisturbed and offer trails for energetic outdoor lovers. Most of the early settlements by the Susquehannock Indians and the Quakers in this area were confined to the river front, since it offered a means of travel and a way to import and export goods.

SUSQUEHANNA BRAVE. This drawing of a Susquehannock Indian is taken from Captain Smith's map of the Chesapeake Bay area *c.* 1608. Smith described this tribe of fierce warriors, believed to be about seven feet tall, as "such great and well-proportioned men . . . Some have cassacks made of beare's heads and skins." (Courtesy of the Historical Society of Harford County.)

10

INDIAN PETROGLYPHS. Above is a drawing of the petroglyphs at Bald Friar *c.* 1880. Although no one is quite certain why the Susquehannocks created these "rock writings," researchers believe that the Native Americans regarded the deep, swift-moving waters of the Susquehanna River with awe. Most of their rock writing has been destroyed, but some was removed before the area was flooded for the building of Conowingo Dam. A few are on display at the Historical Society of Harford County in Bel Air, Maryland. (Courtesy of the Historical Society of Harford County.)

INDIAN PETROGLYPHS. Petroglyphs were found on various islands in the Susquehanna River. In 1916, Martin Kurtz of Jarrettsville and William B. Mayre of the Maryland Historical Society documented and photographed these petroglyphs. In his report *Susquehanna River Expedition*, Mayre suggests these rock writings were carved by the Susquehannocks to "pacify the evil spirit in the bottomless Jacob's Hole." (Courtesy of the Historical Society of Harford County.)

ROCK WRITING. Some people believe the rock writings were works of art. Others think that the connection between the fish shapes in the drawings and the shad that once filled the river illustrates the Susquehannocks' diet of fish and oysters. This is supported by the discovery of large amounts of shells in their places of habitation. (Courtesy of the Historical Society of Harford County.)

SMITH'S FALLES MARKER. This marker was placed near the site where Capt. John Smith encountered "rockes" near present day Lapidum and could not navigate further on the Susquehanna River. Smith and his men disembarked from their ship and continued their exploration on foot to Deer Creek, where they first encountered the Susquehannock Indian tribe. (Courtesy of the Historical Society of Harford County.)

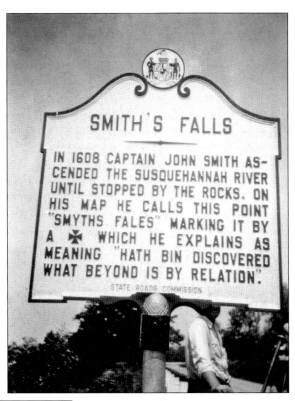

SMITH'S FALLS

IN 1608 CAPTAIN JOHN SMITH AS-
CENDED THE SUSQUEHANNAH RIVER
UNTIL STOPPED BY THE ROCKS. ON
HIS MAP HE CALLS THIS POINT
"SMYTHS FALES" MARKING IT BY
A ✠ WHICH HE EXPLAINS AS
MEANING "HATH BIN DISCOVERED
WHAT BEYOND IS BY RELATION".
STATE ROADS COMMISSION

SMITH'S ROCKS. This view of the Susquehanna River shows rocks protruding above the water line. According to his diary, rocks like this prevented Smith from continuing his journey upriver. (Courtesy of the Historical Society of Harford County.)

13

CONOWINGO VILLAGE. In the language of the Susquehannocks, Conewago means "at the rapids." Numerous petroglyphs were discovered near here at a place called Bald Friar. This village, actually located on the Cecil County side of the river, was flooded when the Conowingo Dam was built in 1926–1928. (Courtesy of the Historical Society of Harford County.)

CONOWINGO BRIDGE. In 1859, this covered bridge was built over the Susquehanna River near Conowingo. It replaced the original bridge that was built in 1820 and destroyed by a flood in 1846. Skirmishes took place here during the Civil War. Federal troops stationed here for three years prevented the Southern armies from crossing into Northern territory. (Courtesy of the Historical Society of Harford County.)

CONOWINGO BRIDGE IN 1910. The covered bridge was destroyed by fire in 1907 and this iron span bridge was built. This bridge was then destroyed by dynamite in 1928 to make way for Conowingo Dam. (Courtesy of the Historical Society of Harford County.)

CONOWINGO MARKER. This roadside marker was erected by the Historical Society of Harford County on Route 1, designating the area of Conowingo near the dam. (Courtesy of the Historical Society of Harford County.)

CONOWINGO DAM. Construction was begun on March 8, 1926, and the dam was operational on March 1, 1928. It was the first major dam built by the Arundel Corporation. A $52 million project under the direction of chief engineer William Eglin, the Conowingo Dam is a concrete gravity dam for hydroelectric power. Its total length is 3,650 feet and its maximum height is 105 feet. The dam supplies electricity to about 300,000 residents of the Philadelphia area. (Courtesy of the Historical Society of Harford County.)

TOWN OF STAFFORD IN 1885. The town was named by Stephen Onion, who owned Rock Forge at Stafford, after Staffordshire, England. Stafford was once a thriving town in the 19th century. Furnaces, forges, mills, and other industries occupied the area. During its prosperous period, Stafford had a store, school, boarding house, and post office. The population of the town fluctuated with the fortunes of the men who owned companies there. Most of the town was destroyed by an ice gorge in 1904. (Courtesy of the Historical Society of Harford County.)

STAFFORD FLINT MILL WORKERS. These mill workers took time out for a photo shoot while balanced on a beam at the Stafford Flint Mill. (Courtesy of the Historical Society of Harford County.)

WRECKING EQUIPMENT. This flint mill equipment was used to crush flint into small stones in preparation for processing into powder. (Courtesy of the Historical Society of Harford County.)

STAFFORD FLINT FURNACE. The furnace was built of Port Deposit granite, assorted stones, and brick. Its total height is 30 feet, and the circular middle portion measures 12 to 15 feet in diameter. The upper section is made of brick and is about 10 feet high and shaped like a beehive. White flint was quarried north of Stafford and brought to the furnace by wagons or canal. The flint was layered with wood and set afire. The heat from the fire drove water out of the flint, reducing it to pebbles. These pebbles were ground into a fine powder, washed, bagged, and sent by canal to Trenton, New Jersey. There it was used to make porcelain pots, pans, and china. (Courtesy of the Historical Society of Harford County.)

STAFFORDSHIRE MILL. This postcard with a photograph of the old Staffordshire Flint Mill was postmarked July 26, 1933, and addressed to E. Allen Hays of Keyser, West Virginia, from "Archer." The inscription reads "Regions around Stafford is a picture of desolation . . . nothing but brambles, underbrush, thickets, pole cats, and snakes." (Courtesy of the Historical Society of Harford County.)

ROCK RUN

ROCK RUN HOUSE, THE HOME OF BRIGADIER-GENERAL JAMES J. ARCHER, WHO RESIGNED FROM THE UNITED STATES ARMY TO JOIN THE CONFEDERACY. WOUNDED AND CAPTURED AT GETTYSBURG JULY I, 1863, GENERAL ARCHER DIED IN RICHMOND OCTOBER 24, 1864, SHORTLY AFTER HIS EXCHANGE.

MARYLAND CIVIL WAR CENTENNIAL COMMISSION

ROCK RUN MARKER. This historical roadside marker commemorates a member of the Archer family, Brig. Gen. James J. Archer, who fought for the Confederacy in the Civil War. He was wounded at the Battle of Gettysburg, imprisoned at Johnson's Island until 1864, and died in Richmond that same year. A comrade once said of Archer, "In his death, Maryland lost one of her most gallant sons, and the Confederacy one of the bravest officers of the Army." (Courtesy of David Duchon.)

ROCK RUN BRIDGE STONE PIERS. The Rock Run Bridge and Banking Company was the first company to construct a bridge across the lower Susquehanna River from Harford to Cecil County. Work on the toll bridge started in 1813 and was completed in 1818. After a fire in 1823, it took five years to rebuild, and the bridge opened for travel in 1828. In 1854, the motion of a herd of cattle being driven too rapidly across the bridge brought down one span. The bridge was again repaired, only to be carried away by ice in the winter of 1856. All that remains of the bridge are the stone piers shown in this photograph. (Courtesy of the Historical Society of Harford County.)

ROCK RUN HOUSE. Also known as the Carter-Archer House, this house was built by John and Rebecca (Harlan) Carter in 1804. John Carter was partners with John Stump in the Rock Run milling business. Carter died in 1805, and Stump purchased the house from Carter's son in 1808 and left it to his daughter, Ann Archer, upon his death in 1816. Ann was married to Dr. John Archer Jr., and the house stayed in their family until the 20th century, when it was sold to the Macklem family in 1904. The Maryland Department of Natural Resources now owns the property. (Courtesy of the Historical Society of Harford County.)

ROCK RUN MILL. This mill has quite an extensive history of ownership. The tract of land was originally called "Land of Promise" and was owned by Jacob Giles, a large landowner in the area. The heirs of Giles's estate sold the half-acre tract to John Stump Jr., who built this mill there in 1794. In 1797, Elizabeth Giles, daughter of Nathaniel Giles, sold 256 acres adjoining the mill to Stump for £750. In 1801, Stump became partners in the milling business with John Carter. Carter died in 1805 and his son sold the half-interest back to Stump in 1808. Upon Stump's death in 1816, the Rock Run Mill property was left to his daughter Ann Archer, wife of Dr. John Archer Jr. Ann Archer lived with her family in the mansion house near the Rock Run Mill until her death in 1867. Her son Henry Archer later acquired the mill property. In 1904, his executors sold the mill to John Macklem for $4,500. Lavinia Macklem, his daughter, deeded the mill and 33 acres to Wilfred Wilkinson in 1929. The property was acquired by the State of Maryland in 1963. (Courtesy of the Historical Society of Harford County.)

ROCK RUN MILL WATERWHEEL. Waterwheels were usually made of wood or iron and had large buckets attached to them. The water from the millrace flowed into the buckets and the weight of the water caused the wheel to turn. This motion turned the grinding machinery inside the mill. (Courtesy of David Duchon.)

ROCK RUN MILL IN DISTANCE AND SMOKEHOUSE ON RIGHT. This early photograph shows the Rock Run Mill on the left and the fish smokehouse on the right. (Courtesy of the Historical Society of Harford County.)

FISH SMOKEHOUSE. When the fishing industry was a thriving business at Lapidum up until the early 20th century, herring was abundant for local consumption as well as for supplying nearby cities on the East Coast. This smoke house was used to process the herring. The herring was salted down in hogsheads and then smoked with hickory logs in the smokehouse. The smokehouse was disassembled in the 1940s by J. Gilman Paul and reassembled at the Steppingstone Museum. (Courtesy of the Historical Society of Harford County.)

WILKINSON MILL RACE. Early dams were constructed of logs, earth, and stone. The water from nearby streams was diverted from the dam to the mill by a "race" or canal. The flow of water was regulated by a gate near the mill. The mill race provided a water source for the numerous mills in the Rock Run–Lapidum area. (Courtesy of the Historical Society of Harford County.)

CAROLA MASON AT WILKINSON DAM. Local resident Carola Mason posed for a photograph at the dam in 1939. Her father Sam Mason was a Darlington farmer and noted Harford County historian and photographer. Many of his glass slides and photographs of Harford County are preserved at the local historical society. (Courtesy of the Historical Society of Harford County.)

BOATING ON THE RIVER AT ROCK RUN. One man and three women, all unidentified, spent a leisurely afternoon boating on the Susquehanna River at Rock Run in 1905. (Courtesy of the Historical Society of Harford County.)

JOHN COOLEY, SCHOOLMASTER.
Cooley served as schoolmaster at Rock
Run School and later as principal at
Darlington School during the late 19th
century. (Courtesy of the Historical
Society of Harford County.)

ROCK RUN SCHOOL. This photograph
of the old schoolhouse on the farm of
Rev. William Stephenson Jr. was taken
in 1897. Records indicate the school was
built *c.* 1825. Stephenson's daughters,
Elizabeth, Hetty, and Hannah, taught
at the school until 1848, when the
new school was built. (Courtesy of the
Historical Society of Harford County.)

STEPHENSON FARM. This is the home of Rev. William Stephenson Jr., minister at Rock Run Church. A revival at his home in 1783 brought about Stephenson's conversion to Methodism. He held Bible readings under the trees for his family and neighbors since the house was too small to accommodate large crowds. By 1810, these gatherings grew so large that the decision was made to build a church. Reverend Stephenson owned slaves but set them free after he converted. (Courtesy of the Historical Society of Harford County.)

ROCK RUN CHURCH. The present-day Rock Run Church at the corner of Rock Run and Craig's Corner Roads was built by Joshua Stevens on land donated by James Stephenson, nephew of the Rev. William Stephenson Jr. The first Rock Run Church was built in 1813, and Stephenson was its first minister. It was used as both a church and a school. Samuel Guild, a schoolmaster from New England, taught school there from "sun up until sundown" and "gave only two weeks holiday during the year." After his death in 1821 the school was abandoned. The stone building served as a church until 1843, when the present building was constructed on a new site to accommodate the increase in membership. (Courtesy of the Historical Society of Harford County.)

LAPIDUM TAVERN. Two gentlemen are pictured taking a break on the porch of the Lapidum Tavern. (Courtesy of the Historical Society of Harford County.)

LAPIDUM HOTEL. This hotel served as a lodging place for weary travelers. It was in close proximity to the ferry and the canal lock at Lapidum. (Courtesy of the Historical Society of Harford County.)

LAPIDUM SCHOOL. This two-story building was used as a school on the lower level and a lodge room upstairs. A deed of March 6, 1870, required that the county transfer the property to Stephenson Lodge when it ceased to be used for school purposes. School was held there until 1945, when the children were transported to Havre de Grace. (Courtesy of the Historical Society of Harford County.)

SUSQUEHANNA TOW PATH. This tow path was a rustic road along the Susquehanna and Tidewater Canal. Three or four mules pulled one or more barges or canal boats as they walked single file along the towpath, averaging a speed of approximately three miles per hour. This 1920 photograph shows mail being delivered by horse and buggy using the old tow path. (Courtesy of the Historical Society of Harford County.)

THE PRESIDENT STOPS FOR TEA. Pres. and Mrs. Warren Harding stopped for tea at the Lapidum teahouse, and the president took time out to feed a small dog. The photograph was taken in 1920, the year of the presidential election. No source could determine the reason for his visit; perhaps it was a stop on the campaign trail. (Courtesy of the Historical Society of Harford County.)

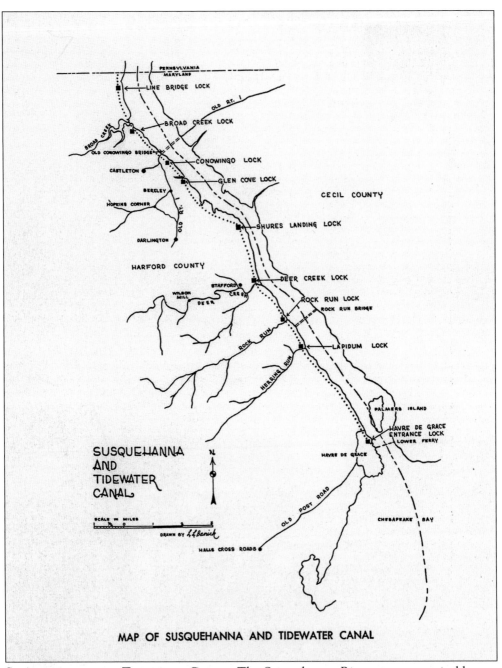

MAP OF SUSQUEHANNA AND TIDEWATER CANAL

SUSQUEHANNA AND TIDEWATER CANAL. The Susquehanna River was not navigable past Lapidum, and the inland roads were virtually impassable during the 19th century. Therefore, the canal was built from Havre de Grace to Wrightsville, Pennsylvania, and was used by early settlers to transport coal, wheat, and timber along the riverfront. The canal measured about 45 miles in length, from 15 to 20 feet in width, and 6 to 12 feet in depth. A total of 29 locks were constructed, nine of which were in Harford County. The locks enabled boats to travel from 20 feet above sea level at Havre de Grace to more than 1,000 feet at Wrightsville. (Courtesy of the Historical Society of Harford County.)

Lapidum Lock No. 9. William Clark was the lock keeper at Lapidum Lock No. 9 in the late 19th century and lived in a house near the lock. As a canal boat approached, the captain blew a conch shell, and the lock keeper operated the necessary gates. When the boat was in the lock, the gates were swung shut. The lower part was opened and water admitted or let out until the boat had reached the new level. (Courtesy of the Historical Society of Harford County.)

Canal. Floods were destructive to canals and repairs were expensive. Also, railroad lines entered the region and took some of the trade from the canal. In 1890, the upper part of the lock system was abandoned. (Courtesy of the Historical Society of Harford County.)

ICE GORGE, 1904. The waters of the Susquehanna remained relatively calm except during times of flooding from the spring thaw. The river then became turbulent and destructive for the small towns on its banks, as it carried huge pieces of ice right to their front doors. (Courtesy of the Historical Society of Harford County.)

ICE GORGE ON THE SUSQUEHANNA. Ice gorges were frequent prior to the building of the Conowingo Dam. They were annual occurrences that brought devastation and ruin such as this to Lapidum. (Courtesy of the Historical Society of Harford County.)

VIEW OF THE ICE GORGE IN LAPIDUM. The Lapidum Hotel escaped damage during this ice gorge, as it sat on higher ground; however, the rest of the town was not so fortunate. The ice gorges destroyed homes and businesses in the small town along the river. (Courtesy of the Historical Society of Harford County.)

ICE GORGE CLOSES THE ROAD AT LAPIDUM. The road through Lapidum was virtually impassable during times of ice gorges. The ice jams ranged from 15 to 20 feet in height. Residents had no choice but to leave their homes when the spring thaw turned into floods. (Courtesy of the Historical Society of Harford County.)

VIEW OF SUSQUEHANNA, 1905. This postcard depicts a calm Susquehanna River in 1905. This is quite a contrast to the postcard below, showing the ice gorge. Prior to the building of the Conowingo Dam, ice gorges were common and wreaked havoc on the riverside communities. (Courtesy of the Historical Society of Harford County.)

FISH SHEDS IN THE ICE GORGE. This photograph was taken looking north up the Susquehanna River from Havre de Grace towards Lapidum. Note the old railroad bridge in the background. Fish sheds were damaged during the ice gorges, but children saw the huge chunks of ice as a playground. On the left in the distance is the lock house at the Susquehanna and Tidewater Canal. (Courtesy of the Historical Society of Harford County.)

Steamer "Susquehanna," near Port Deposit, Md.

STEAMBOAT *SUSQUEHANNA*. From 1840 to 1900, regular steamboat service existed on the Chesapeake Bay from Baltimore up the Susquehanna River as far as Lapidum. Steamboats that offered this service were the *Canton*, the *Ferry*, and the *City Belle*. This postcard was addressed to Miss Mildred Bortner of 249 West Market Street in York, Pennsylvania, from "Katherine." It bears a 1¢ stamp and was postmarked at Cape Henry in Norfolk, Virginia, on December 9, 1911, at 6:30 p.m. (Courtesy of the Historical Society of Harford County.)

STEAMER *SUSQUEHANNA* NEAR PORT DEPOSIT. This postcard was addressed to Mrs. M. Laffy of Hanover, in Howard County, Maryland, from "Estella" with the inscription "I would rather be on water than on land." It was postmarked in Port Deposit on July 29, 1908. With improvements in passenger transportation by railroad, service by boat in this area declined. The burning of the *City Belle* at Havre de Grace in 1900 marked the end of regular steamboat service. (Courtesy of the Historical Society of Harford County.)

Two

FISHING ON THE SUSQUEHANNA

During the 18th and early 19th centuries, commercial fishermen operated from shore and built fish houses at Lapidum to cure and process thousands of barrels of fish for shipment to cities on the East Coast. Herring from the Susquehanna River became well known, and Conestoga wagons traveled from York, Harrisburg, and other cities to pick up fresh fish at Lapidum. By 1820, advancements were made in fishing methods, and fish floats were built and anchored in mid-stream during the spawning season. The fishing trade provided employment for many local residents, migrant workers, and even hoboes who wandered through the region. The building of the Conowingo Dam in 1928 brought an end to commercial fishing on the Susquehanna River, and in the present day, fishing on the river is solely a recreational activity, not a way of life.

BOUNTY OF FISH. As early as 1652, the Susquehanna Indians obtained fishing rights at the mouth of the Susquehanna River by treaty with Annapolis. John Smith recorded in his diary, "Abundance of fish lying so thicke with their heads above the water, as for want of nets, our barge running against them, we attempted to catch them in frying pans; but found we had a bad instrument to catch fish with." (Courtesy of Steppingstone Museum Archives.)

FISH FLOAT. Invented by Asahel Bailey of Havre de Grace, a fish float was usually about 75 feet long and was built of logs with a wooden floor. The float provided small sheds or "shacks" as living quarters for the itinerant fishermen who stayed there for the six-week fishing season. Each float had a large kitchen and storage bins for fish and food. A steam engine was placed at either end of the float to provide power for hauling in the nets. One side of the float, about 50 feet in width, sloped down into the water and served as a landing deck for the fish. On this float, there is a shad house on the right and scows are tied up on the left. (Courtesy of Steppingstone Museum Archives.)

READYING THE SEINE. Fishermen check the seine (large net) in preparation for another day of fishing. (Courtesy of Steppingstone Museum Archives.)

LOADING THE NETS ON BOARD. The nets were loaded on board a scow to be hauled out into the river. (Courtesy of Steppingstone Museum Archives.)

LAYING OUT THE SEINE. These fishermen lay out the mile-long seine with corks at the top and weights at the bottom. (Courtesy of Steppingstone Museum Archives.)

HAULING IN THE NETS. As soon as the oarsmen finished laying out the seine, the net was hauled in from both ends. The lead line was brought up first, and then the cork line was brought up over that. (Courtesy of Steppingstone Museum Archives.)

A GOOD CATCH. The fish were dumped on the float's large apron to be cleaned and sorted. (Courtesy of Steppingstone Museum Archives.)

UNLOADING THE FISH. The fishermen had lots of cleaning and sorting to do at this point. (Courtesy of Steppingstone Museum Archives.)

NO FISH STORY. Abundant catches of herring and shad such as this were a daily occurrence at Lapidum. (Courtesy of Steppingstone Museum Archives.)

CLEANING THE FISH. The catch was sorted, cleaned, and loaded into open-weave baskets. (Courtesy of Steppingstone Museum Archives.)

FILLING THE BASKETS. Cleaned fish were loaded into baskets to be taken to shore for packing or smoking. Fishermen were paid with "checks," or tokens per basket. (Courtesy of Steppingstone Museum Archives.)

A SCOW. Approximately 20 feet in length, scows were manned by 16 oarsmen. The Black Diamond motor boat, a later invention, replaced the scows and oarsmen in the early 1920s. (Courtesy of Steppingstone Museum Archives.)

PHOTO TIME. Families and friends sometimes visited the fishermen for a social outing. An unidentified woman with a box camera had fun snapping photographs of everyone on this occasion. (Courtesy of Steppingstone Museum Archives.)

SAY "FISH." The camera captured the antics of this young man standing behind the couple. The gentleman seated on the left is a fisherman. Because of the way the others are dressed, it is safe to assume they were visitors on board the float. (Courtesy of Steppingstone Museum Archives.)

FAMILIES AND FRIENDS VISIT. Everyone dressed up for the occasion and posed for this group photograph on the fishing float. (Courtesy of Steppingstone Museum Archives.)

CATCH OF THE DAY. Two unidentified men proudly displayed some rather large fish for this photo opportunity. (Courtesy of Steppingstone Museum Archives.)

ANOTHER DAY DONE. This gentleman was nicely dressed, but it is unknown why he wore a cap similar to a bonnet. The men in the background are loading the seine on board the scow for the next fishing trip. (Courtesy of Steppingstone Museum Archives.)

MOTHER AND CHILDREN VISIT THE RIVER. Families enjoyed going to the river for an afternoon, sometimes visiting relatives who worked on the fishing floats. (Courtesy of Steppingstone Museum Archives.)

BABY AT THE RIVERSIDE. This mother, with her baby in the pram, relaxed on a sunny afternoon by the Susquehanna. (Courtesy of Steppingstone Museum Archives.)

Three

THE MACKLEM FAMILY

In 1882, John Montgomery Macklem, born October 17, 1837, purchased the land in what is now Susquehanna State Park. He married Mary Elizabeth Davies and built a home for his family on Rock Run Road near Rock Run Church. He also built a home at Quaker Bottom Farm for his eight daughters, referred to as "the aunties:" Elizabeth, Mary, Lavinia, Anna, Rebecca, Lucy, Sarah, and Bessie. The Macklems also had two sons. William operated one of the farms for his father before moving to Easton, Maryland, to manage canning houses. John Wesley Macklem helped manage Quaker Bottom Farm and lived there with his wife Jennie and two daughters, Mary and Madeline, until his death in 1939. The aunties sold a tract of land to John Gilman Paul, a lawyer from Baltimore, and that tract is the location of the Steppingstone Museum.

MARY MACKLEM ON A HORSE. Mary Macklem lived at Quaker Bottom Farm with her parents, John Wesley and Jennie Macklem, and her sister Madeline. Even at the young age of five, horseback riding was one of her favorite pastimes.

JOHN MONTGOMERY MACKLEM. Macklem and his wife Mary moved to Quaker Bottom Farm from the New Castle, Delaware, area about 1882. He acquired the farm from his brother-in-law, Jacob Stilwell, for partial payment of a debt. In this *c.* 1909 photo, Macklem reads the newspaper while relaxing in his favorite chair at the farm. (Courtesy of Mary Macklem Peal and family.)

MARY ELIZABETH DAVIES. The Macklems had 10 children: two boys in addition to the eight girls known as the aunties. Mary and her husband John moved to Quaker Bottom Farm when their son John Wesley was eight. This photograph was taken in 1913. (Courtesy of Mary Macklem Peal and family.)

JOHN WESLEY MACKLEM IN 1901. John Wesley was born on November 20, 1875. He and his wife Jennie managed the mill and lived in the mill house for a short time before he came down with malaria. They moved to Delaware, and then returned to Quaker Bottom Farm in 1909. He remained there until his death in May 1939. (Courtesy of Mary Macklem Peal and family.)

JENNIE ESTELLE WILKINSON IN 1901. Jennie Wilkinson was born on May 4, 1882, and died on July 18, 1967. She married John Wesley Macklem and they had two daughters, Madeline and Mary. They lived at Quaker Bottom Farm. (Courtesy of Mary Macklem Peal and family.)

THE MACKLEM HOUSE IN 1909. This house, built by John M. Macklem, is still standing on Quaker Bottom Road across from the aunties' house. The Macklem family lived here from 1909 to 1942. The house has undergone renovations and additions by its present owners. (Courtesy of Mary Macklem Peal and family.)

THE MACKLEM GIRLS RIDING IN STYLE. Madeline (behind the wheel) and Mary (passenger) wore goggles as they took a test drive in their father's Caddy. This 1911 Cadillac was the first automobile purchased by their father John W. Macklem. Note the steering wheel is on the right side. (Courtesy of Mary Macklem Peal and family.)

MARY'S FIRST DAY OF SCHOOL, 1910. Mary Macklem attended Harford Seminary School, a one-room schoolhouse on Webster Road, from the first through sixth grades. She remembers making the one-mile walk during good weather and being chauffeured by her neighbors, the Miller family, in a buggy pulled by a white horse named Jenny during inclement weather. The school is now a private residence. (Courtesy of Mary Macklem Peal and family.)

MARY'S 1917 SCHOOL PICTURE.
This is a class photograph of Mary Macklem, who was born February 3, 1904 in Nottingham, Pennsylvania. Her family moved to her grandparents' farm in 1909. (Courtesy of Mary Macklem Peal and family.)

SCHOOL DAYS AT HARFORD SEMINARY, 1915. Pictured from left to right are the following: (first row) Purnell Knight, Dena Brinkman, Leon Thompson, Dorothy Brinkman, Frank Dormicack, unidentified, Armfield Carlile, Elbern Thompson, and John Dormicack; (second row) Willard DeBaugh, Harry Rider, Armfield Mitchell, Marion Brinkman, unidentified, Madeline Macklem, and Daniel Rider; (third row) Winifred Carlile, Eva DeBaugh, Mary Macklem, Rebecca Mitchell, and ? Laurence; (fourth row) Edna Carlile, Mary Strong, Sarah DeBaugh, and Lena DeBaugh; (fifth row) John Fahey, Mildred Laurence, Lillian DeBaugh, and Helen Christy. (Courtesy of Mary Macklem Peal and family.)

MARY ON MISSY, 1918. Horseback riding was one of Mary Macklem's favorite pastimes when all the farm chores were completed. In addition to household chores, Mary worked in her father's canning house during the summer months, where she ran the corn husking machine. (Courtesy of Mary Macklem Peal and family.)

HAVRE DE GRACE HIGH SCHOOL, 1918. Pictured from left to right are the following: (first row) Miriam Miller, Dorothy Gaffey, Marion Barrett, Mary Macklem, Virna Rutter, Mary Quirk, Jennie Amato, and Katherine Taylor; (second row) James Prevas, Julia Phol, Evelyn Arnold, Mildred Knight, Louise Klair, Louise White, Lucile White, and Margaret Curren; (third row) Charles Prescott, Arnold Pfaffenback, Edward Colburn, Henry Lily, Daniel Rider, Eldon Leithiser, and Herbert Colburn. (Courtesy of Mary Macklem Peal and family.)

WILLIAM PEAL, 1919. This photo shows a member of the Havre de Grace football team. After high school, William Peal became captain of police at Union Station in Washington, D.C. He married Mary Macklem in November, 1924, in Baltimore, and the couple took the train to Niagara Falls for their honeymoon. Mary and William had three daughters, Miriam, Ferol, and Mary, and a son who died in infancy. (Courtesy of Mary Macklem Peal and family.)

HAVRE DE GRACE SOCCER TEAM, 1919. This photograph of the Havre de Grace soccer team was taken at Baltimore's Patterson Park in 1919. Pictured from left to right are the following: (first row) Joseph Haut, Kenneth Miller, Eldon Leithiser, Louis Backy, and William Peal; (second row) #1 Joseph Fahey, #2 James Prevas, #3 Myles Thorphy, #4 James Harlow, #5 Henry Lilly, #6 Sydney Schrader, #7 Robert Harlow, #8 Dail Currier, and #9 Professor Owens. (Courtesy of Mary Macklem Peal and family.)

MILLARD J. TYDINGS. This photo shows former Maryland governor Millard J. Tydings (front passenger side, at left) out for a ride with Seth Peal (driver). Robert Gorsuch is seated at right in the back seat, next to an unidentified passenger. Seth Peal was the father of William Peal, who married Mary Macklem. Seth ran a small boat-repair shop along the waterfront in Havre de Grace. (Courtesy of Mary Macklem Peal and family.)

CROQUET ANYONE? Croquet players took a break for this photo shoot on June 17, 1899, at Garland, Maryland (now Rock Run). Pictured from left to right are the following: (first row) Spencer Springer, lying down; (second row) Belle Coale Cooley, Janie Martin, Jennie Wilkinson Macklem, Miss Stiegler, and Anne Martin; (third row) Walker Wilkinson, Vernon Wilkinson, Lucinda Walker Wilkinson, and Virdin Martin. (Courtesy of Mary Macklem Peal and family.)

THE WALKER BROTHERS, 1860. Pictured from left to right are the following: (sitting) Augustus Walker and George Walker; (standing) Robert Walker, John Walker, Jacob Walker, Christian Walker, and Charles Walker. (Courtesy of Mary Macklem Peal and family.)

THE WALKER FAMILY. Pictured are, from left to right, Nellie Walker Carter, Rebecca Walker Wilkinson, Robert Walker, and Lucinda Walker Wilkinson. The photograph was taken at the Wilkinsons' house near Rock Run Church *c.* 1912. (Courtesy of Mary Macklem Peal and family.)

GEORGE WILKINSON, 1906.
George, father of Jennie
Wilkinson Macklem, lived in
a stone house near Rock Run
Church. He was an avid hunter
and is shown here with the
rewards of a day in the field.
(Courtesy of Mary Macklem Peal
and family.)

HAULING TOMATOES TO THE CANNING HOUSE. Armann Bowman worked for the Macklems
on Quaker Bottom Farm. He is shown here with a team of mules pulling a wagon full of tomatoes
to the canning house in the distance. Only the foundation of the canning house remains today.
Note the black snake whip in his hand. (Courtesy of Nelson Bowman.)

CANNING LABEL. John Montgomery Macklem canned only tomatoes in his canning house at Quaker Bottom Farm. He called his tomatoes "Bessie Brand Tomatoes," as shown on this label. (Courtesy of Bernie Bodt.)

CANNING LABEL. John Wesley Macklem canned both tomatoes and corn. His daughter, Mary Macklem, ran the corn-husking machine. After being weighed on a scale, the corn was placed in a machine to remove the husks. Working there was a hot and dusty job in August and September of each year. This was Macklem's label for Spring Valley Brand Tomatoes. (Courtesy of Bernie Bodt.)

Four

FAMILY LIFE IN LEVEL-WEBSTER

The small community of Level received its name from an original land grant called "Rich Level" consisting of 1,915 acres in the Hopewell neighborhood patented to George Yates in 1672. Records indicate it was named due to the path of commerce that crossed the Susquehanna River at Rock Run and climbed the hill from the river to "level" land. Later, when a village grew in the area, the name was shortened to just Level. Not too much has changed in this quiet community. A modern volunteer fire station was built to accommodate the population growth in the surrounding areas, and the Level Garage and an antique shop in the old Bradfield Country Store are still open for business. The sounds of the blacksmith at the anvil and the farmer driving teams of oxen up the road are heard no more, but the small-town feeling and friendliness still linger in the community.

MR. FOARD AT THE BLACKSMITH SHOP. William Lorenzo "Bill" Foard stands in the doorway of the blacksmith shop built by his father Edson Foard in 1883. Foard's shop "survived wars, depressions, and taxes" for almost 100 years, and Bill Foard practiced his trade until the age of 96. After his death, the shop was moved to Steppingstone Museum to be preserved as part of the local farm museum. (Courtesy of Steppingstone Museum Archives.)

THE FOARD BLACKSMITH SHOP. This postcard shows the shop in Level built by Edson Foard in 1883. Bill Foard and his brother Charles took over the business in 1909 after their father's death. Charles handled the bookkeeping and Bill operated the shop until his death in May 1981. The back part of the shop, known as the wareroom, was used to register voters and served as a voting precinct from 1892 to 1958. In 1983, Foard's daughter Marguerite donated the shop to Steppingstone Museum (Courtesy of Robert Janssen.)

THE FOARD BLACKSMITH SHOP. In the forge area, on the hard-packed earthen floor, twin forges stand like monuments to the trade. The walls of the shop have wide-beamed, pitted oak planks and there are wide spaces between the boards that made the room damp and drafty at times. The pot-bellied stove, known to build a good fire, was the focal point of the back storeroom, where visitors stepped in to pass the time of day with Bill Foard. (Courtesy of Steppingstone Museum Archives.)

BILL FOARD. Born in Level, Foard spent his entire 96 years there and learned the blacksmith trade in the shop his father built. He often said that he began working in the shop as soon as he was tall enough to see over the anvil. Blacksmiths were experts in welding, tempering ax blades, making horseshoes, cutting and shrinking tires for a wagon or buggy, and building wagon beds. (Courtesy of Steppingstone Museum Archives.)

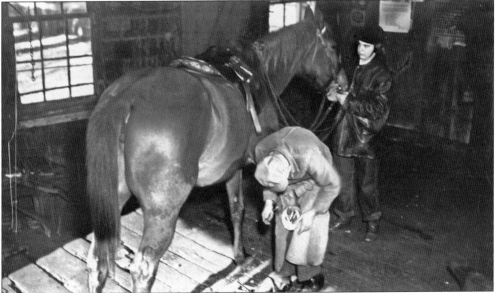

BILL FOARD SHOEING A HORSE. Horseshoes are very important to protect the hooves from injury. Shoes were attached with a special nail driven through the outer part of the hoof. The charge for shoeing a horse in the early 20th century was $2 per horse. Approximately 15 to 20 horses a day were shod in the shop. For icy roads in winter, horses were shod with ice shoes that had cleats similar to baseball or track shoes. During one week in one icy winter, 130 horses came through the shop for ice shoes. Foard is seen here shoeing a horse, while its owner, Ann Stewart, watches the process. (Courtesy of Steppingstone Museum Archives.)

FIRST WOMAN VOTER IN LEVEL. In 1920, May Bradfield, wife of store owner Oscar Bradfield, was the first woman voter in Level. From 1892 through 1958, Harford County elections were held at the Foard Blacksmith Shop in the big wareroom. In 1958, the rent was $20 a day. On November 13 of that same year, a letter was sent to the *Havre de Grace Record* by Mrs. William E. Fletcher on Chapel Road near Havre de Grace complaining about the conditions at this location. She thought voters were entitled to a more up-to-date place to vote. As a result of this letter, Bill Foard notified the board of elections to find another location. In 1960, the elections were held at the Level Fire Company firehouse, where the rent remained $20 a day. (Courtesy of Steppingstone Museum Archives.)

LEVEL VOLUNTEER FIRE STATION. This postcard shows the old Level Volunteer Fire Station with two bays for equipment. A larger fire station and hall replaced this one. Community volunteers donate their time to run the station. (Courtesy of Robert Janssen.)

CENTENARY CHURCH. This was the original name of the Hopewell United Methodist Church. Centenary Church was built in 1866 on a one-acre lot owned by George Walker. Walker had purchased the land from Harvey Mitchell, who stipulated in the deed "that no hogs or chickens were to be kept on the place." Walker informed Mitchell that a church would be built on the site. Rev. Thomas Lee was minister of the Susquehanna Circuit when the church was built. (Courtesy of Nelson Bowman.)

HOPEWELL UNITED METHODIST CHURCH. Rev. John Buchheister, pastor in 1955, proposed a building program for the construction of a new church. A ground-breaking ceremony was held on May 21, 1962, and construction was completed by Andrew Pasqualini in December 1962. The total construction cost was $98,167. This new brick church was built next to the wooden frame structure, which was later torn down. The congregation moved into the building, with Rev. William Miller as their pastor, on January 13, 1963. (Courtesy of Isabelle Stearn.)

BOWMAN-TAYLOR HOUSE. This log and frame structure was built around 1800 on Level Road. The oldest section served as an inn on the Baltimore-Philadelphia Road. A Level resident related an amusing story about "Chic the Tomato Pic," who lived in an outbuilding on the property. Chic would pick tomatoes every summer and "when the tomatoes were gone, so was Chic." (Courtesy of Isabelle Stearn.)

STEARN'S STORE. Leonard Stearn and wife Annie ran this general store in Level. The name of the store was L. W. Stearn General Merchandise and Harness Supplies, and its slogan was "You'll Have to Scratch Some to Match our Prices." Standing on the porch are, from left to right, Lionel Duff, Leonard Stearn, an unidentified boy, Hazel Stearn, an unidentified boy, and Leonard Stearn Jr. (Courtesy of Nelson Bowman.)

HARNESSMAKER. Mr. McQuen ran the harness shop, which was located next to Stearn's store. He later opened a harness shop on Pratt Street in Baltimore. (Courtesy of Isabelle Stearn.)

OSCAR BRADFIELD, ENTREPRENEUR. In 1924, Oscar Bradfield gave up farming and bought a store from Nelson Cooper. The store was moved by a team of oxen from its original location at Rock Run and Darlington Roads. George Bradfield and his wife, Emma, took over the operation after Oscar's death in 1958. At one time, the store stocked coal and other commodities and stayed open as late as 10:00 or 11:00 p.m. The owners also extended credit to their customers, whose accounts were paid up every Friday night. With rising competition from larger stores, the Bradfields decided to cut their hours and sell mostly groceries and a few necessities. The store finally closed in the early 1980s. (Courtesy of Isabelle Stearn.)

BRADFIELD'S STORE. This postcard shows Level's traditional country store sometime before it closed in the 1980s. An antique shop occupies the building today. (Courtesy of Robert Janssen.)

BROTHERLY LOVE. Alfred Bowman (left) and his brother James, both born and raised in the Webster area, posed for this early photograph. (Courtesy of Elma Bowman.)

ELMA BOWMAN AND THE TWINS. Elma, wife of Alfred Bowman, is shown here with their twins, Ann and Alfred, at two years of age. (Courtesy of Elma Bowman.)

ANN AND ALFRED BOWMAN. The twin children of Elma and Alfred Bowman are about nine months old in this photo. Ann, seated in the old-fashioned baby walker/bouncer doesn't seem too happy. Alfred seems a little unsure about sitting in what looks like a big bowl. (Courtesy of Elma Bowman.)

ANN BOWMAN AND PLAYMATES. Ann Bowman seems undecided about getting too close to the big rooster. (Courtesy of Elma Bowman.)

FAMILIES AND FRIENDS. Pictured standing in the back row on the right is Alfred Bowman. His father Armon kneels in front of him. (Courtesy of Elma Bowman.)

WOMEN WITH CHILDREN. Elma Bowman (right) is shown holding one of the twins, Ann. Her mother-in-law, Anna Bowman, is in the middle holding Alfred. The woman and child on the left are unidentified. (Courtesy of Elma Bowman.)

LENORA CLARENCE ELY BOWMAN, 1893–1923.
This young woman died at the age of 30 from tuberculosis. It was believed that she contracted the disease from milk. She left two small children, Nelson and Mayfield, who were raised by their grandmother. Mayfield passed away in 1984, and Nelson still lives in the area, not far from his birthplace. (Courtesy of Nelson Bowman.)

BROTHER AND SISTER. Nelson Bowman, age 3; and his sister Mayfield, age 9, are shown here near Bradfield's Store shortly after the death of their mother, Lenora Ely Bowman. The children were raised by Olivia Carr Bowman. At one time, their grandfather, Warren Nelson Bowman, owned most of the land where Level is located today. (Courtesy of Nelson Bowman.)

STREET BOWMAN'S CATCH OF THE DAY, 1942. Level resident and past Harford Country treasurer Street Bowman is pictured here with his catch of the day, rockfish. This photograph was taken in front of Bradfield's Store and shows Bowman's 1936 Ford. Bowman and his fishing buddies took day trips to Bowers Beach in Delaware and brought back "washtubs full of fish" and gave them to everyone in the community. (Courtesy of Isabelle Stearn.)

ELNORA BOWMAN. In this 1947 photograph, Elnora Elsner, age 29, stands in front of a 1936 Pontiac belonging to her brother-in-law, Alfred Bowman. Elnora was the twin sister of Elma Bowman, wife of Alfred. In 1954, Elnora married Nelson Bowman, cousin of Alfred. One could say they had strong family ties. (Courtesy of Elma Bowman.)

EASTER EGG HUNT. Families in the Level-Webster community gathered for an Easter egg hunt on Easter Monday, April 8, 1947. The photograph was taken at Augusta Elsner's home on Webster Road. (Courtesy of Elma Bowman.)

SCHOOL DAYS. Ann and Alfred Bowman Jr., with their cousin, Bay Himes (right), are ready for school. (Courtesy of Elma Bowman.)

HAY RAKERS. Nelson Bowman Sr., Harry Bailey, and Joe Sampson raked hay on Locust Hill Farm, down the road from Level. They are pictured here in the 1940s with their wagon and hay forks. (Courtesy of Nelson Bowman.)

HORSES GRAZING. The Bowmans' horses Maude (front) and the little one Lady lazily graze in the field. (Courtesy of Nelson Bowman.)

THE CLASS OF 1921 AT PROSPECT SCHOOL WITH MISS DONNA B. JOHNSON. This stone schoolhouse may have been built as early as 1850. It is located on Darlington Road on the way from the community of Hopewell-Level to Harmony Church. The building is hexagon shaped, with a window in five sides and the door in the other. Courthouse records show that "this lot, 87 perches of ground, was purchased by the School Commissioners on October 8, 1850 from William Brown and wife for use as a school." The stone building ceased to be used as a school in 1930, when it was purchased by the late Wiley Martin. It is still used today as a dwelling. Only the teacher, Miss Johnson (third from left in the back row) can be positively identified. (Courtesy of Harford County Historical Society.)

PROSPECT SCHOOL STUDENTS. A group of students is pictured in front of the Prospect School. The year is not known, but the children are holding a 48-star American flag, so it was probably prior to the admittance of Alaska and Hawaii. (Courtesy of Harford County Historical Society.)

ALDINO SCHOOL CLASS C. 1926. Pictured from left to right are the following: (first row) Herbie Atkinson, ? Beal, Cornett Williamson, and Eddie Rumsey; (second row) Leonard Stearn Jr., Harry Atkinson, Armon Bowman, Earl Atkinson, George Walter, Jack Hopkins, Nelson Bowman, and Jack Coale; (third row) Irene Estes, unidentified, Edna Blakely, Marjorie Hopkins, Verna Cooper, Marguerite Foard, Nancy Vincent, unidentified, Miriam Walker, Francis Worthington, Mildred Stearn, Jane Viele, and Vivian Lee; (fourth row) Ruth Williamson, unidentified, Mary Libby Taylor, Thelma Hopkins, Dorothy Rumsey, and Sara Bowman; (fifth row) Miss Sale, Rita May Estes, Ariel Walker, unidentified, Alfred Bowman, Anita Rumsey, and Mary Virginia Cooper. (Courtesy of Nelson Bowman.)

ELSNER'S CANNERY AT WEBSTER. This aerial view shows the Elsner property on Webster Road. The Elsner Canning House is the large building on the left. The old family homestead on the right still stands and remains a dwelling. However, the canning house and outbuildings are no more. From 1909 to 1931, Harry W. Elsner operated the canning house there. After his death, his wife Augusta continued the operation into the 1950s. (Courtesy of Pat and Art Elsner.)

CANNERY WORKERS. Canning was a prosperous industry in Harford County from the late 19th to the mid-20th century. These women worked in the Elsner Canning House, peeling and packing tomatoes. Working in the cannery usually involved 10–12 hour workdays during the hot summer months of August and September. (Courtesy of Pat and Art Elsner.)

HANGING OUT AT THE CANNING HOUSE. The Rakowski sisters, Rose (left) and Patricia (right), stand in front of baskets filled with tomatoes at the Elsner Canning House. The tomatoes had been brought in from the field on the wagon to the canning house for processing. The Rakowski sisters' grandmother, Olvenia Pruett, worked in the canning house. (Courtesy of Pat and Art Elsner.)

AUGUSTA ELSNER, CANNERY OPERATOR. Augusta Elsner and hired hand Mr. Topper stand in front of a Farm-All F-12 tractor at the Elsner Canning House. After her husband's death in 1935, Augusta operated the Elsner Canning House in Webster. (Courtesy of Elma Bowman.)

ELSNER CANNING LABEL. Pictured is the label for Fair Hill fancy cut stringless beans. (Courtesy of Pat and Art Elsner.)

FARMDALE TOMATOES

Delicious served cold right from the can or heated and seasoned with Louella Butter, salt, pepper and sugar. Excellent in dishes containing meat or fish, with spaghetti, macaroni, hominy or rice, or in combination with many vegetables. Often used for making Tomato Soup or Tomato Sauce.

Size of can .... No. 2
Net weight .... 1 lb. 3 oz.
Cups .... Approx. 2½
Servings .... 4 to 5

BAKED TOMATOES WITH ONIONS

No. 2 can Farmdale Tomatoes   1 tablespoon Louella Butter
3 large onions   salt—pepper

Place a layer of Farmdale Tomatoes in a baking dish, season with salt and pepper and dot with a teaspoon of butter. Arrange a layer of sliced onions on the tomatoes then repeat, having two layers of onions and three of tomatoes. Cover and bake in a moderate oven (350 degrees) 45 to 60 minutes or until onions are tender. 5 to 6 servings.

NET WEIGHT 1 LB. 3 OZ.

ELSNER CANNING LABEL. The Elsners used this label for their Farmdale tomatoes. (Courtesy of Nelson Bowman.)

Five

A PLACE TO CALL HOME

Many historic houses still grace the land around Susquehanna State Park near Havre de Grace. Some have withstood the test of time for over two centuries. Many of the houses have remained in one family since their ancestors first settled this area. Familiar family names in the area are Archer, Cooley, Giles, Silver, Smith, Stephenson, and Stump. They operated ferries, fisheries, and mills, and some were active civic or religious leaders in the community. Families took pride in restoring their old homes; however, some have been passed on to newcomers and subjected to renovations. Most of the houses shown in this section are listed on the National Register.

GILES FARMHOUSE AT LAND OF PROMISE. The Steppingstone farmhouse at Land of Promise was built *c.* 1771 by Nathaniel Giles. Coming from an enterprising Quaker family, Giles was a large landowner, planter, and prosperous merchant in the area. He lived here with his wife, Sarah Hammond, and five daughters until his death in 1775. (Courtesy of Steppingstone Museum.)

EIGHTRUPP. The Perkins family owned this land, called Eightrupp, on Quaker Bottom Road in the late 18th century. During that time, Perkins ran the ferry line at Lapidum. The stone and stucco house was built in "telescopic" style on a terraced slope. The frame section that connects the two buildings was probably added by Benjamin Silver. The property is now owned by the State of Maryland Department of Natural Resources. (Courtesy of Chris Weeks Collection, Historical Society of Harford County.)

BOTTS-WORTHINGTON HOUSE. This cottage and the house at Land of Promise (Steppingstone Museum) are mirror images of each other. The 1798 tax list indicates that John Hall Hughes owned the land. The stone house, measuring 30 feet by 25 feet, was occupied by the tenant "widow Touchstone." The house is now unoccupied and almost in ruin. (Courtesy of Chris Weeks Collection, Historical Society of Harford County.)

THE "BIRD HOUSE." This stone house received its name when it was owned by the Maryland Ornithological Society in the early- to mid-20th century. The land was owned by Samuel Gover in the late 18th century, and Gover's daughters Elizabeth, Margaret, Hannah, Susan, and Caroline ran a boarding school there, the Gover Seminary, which was destroyed by a fire in 1825. The Archer family of Rock Run later owned the house and used it as a tenant house, before it was acquired by the Maryland Department of Natural Resources. (Courtesy of Chris Weeks Collection, Historical Society of Harford County.)

FOURTEEN SHILLINGS. The Thomas family of Rock Run is believed to have built the center log section of this house in the first decade of the 19th century. Since that time, the house has undergone many alterations. In 1836, the Cooley family enlarged the dwelling, and it remained in that family until the early 20th century. It is unclear why this house is called 14 Shillings. (Courtesy of Chris Weeks Collection, Historical Society of Harford County.)

MOUNT FRIENDSHIP. This Georgian mansion was built in the 1770s by Samuel Thomas, a prosperous Quaker in the Rock Run area. Thomas's granddaughter Amanda Jarrett and her husband, Abraham, renovated the house in 1821. Mount Friendship remained in the Thomas-Jarrett-Cooley family until 1939. It is now owned and occupied by Mrs. Frederick Viele Jr. (Courtesy of Chris Weeks Collection, Historical Society of Harford County.)

SMITH FERRY HOUSE. Thomas Smith was ferry operator at Lapidum and built this house, also known as the Watts-Virdin House, *c.* 1790 or earlier. Albert P. Silver's 1888 history *Lapidum* records that, "During the Revolution, Smith ferried French troops across the river on their way to Yorktown." The house passed through the Bell and Stump families prior to Dr. Virdin purchasing the property in 1856. (Courtesy of Chris Weeks Collection, Historical Society of Harford County.)

THOMAS SMITH HOUSE. Thomas Smith II, grandson of Thomas Smith, the ferryman (who died in 1791), purchased a 160-acre tract from his father Nathaniel in 1838 and built this frame house. The property remained in the Smith family until the 1940s. (Courtesy of Chris Weeks Collection, Historical Society of Harford County.)

STEPHENSON-ARCHER HOUSE. Also known as Hygeia Hall, this house served as the summer home of Dr. John Archer Jr. and his wife, Ann Stump Archer. They purchased the land from Rev. William Stephenson in 1824. The Archers traveled about a mile or so from their home at Rock Run to this house on Wilkinson Road to escape the summer heat. (Courtesy of Chris Weeks Collection, Historical Society of Harford County.)

JAMES STEPHENSON HOUSE. The brother of Rev. William Stephenson Jr., James Stephenson built this house on Craigs Corner Road in 1797. Reverend Stephenson built Rock Run Church on donated land that was part of this farm. This house remained in the Stephenson family until 1902. (Courtesy of Chris Weeks Collection, Historical Society of Harford County.)

TODD STEPHENSON HOUSE. Reverend Stephenson, who founded the Masonic lodge in Lapidum and was connected with Rock Run Church, lived here in the mid-20th century. Prior to that, the property belonged to the Thomas family of Mount Friendship and to the Cooley family. The construction of the two-story granite house, also known as the Stephenson-Hopkins House, is credited to stonemason Joshua Stevens, c. 1940. (Courtesy of Chris Weeks Collection, Historical Society of Harford County.)

GOLDEN VEIN FARM. Located on Lapidum Road, this house is one of several once owned by the Hughes family. In 1878, Evan Hughes lived here. Although the house has recent renovations, the kitchen wing dates to 1800, and the five-bay main section dates to the late 19th century. It is still a private residence. (Courtesy of Chris Weeks Collection, Historical Society of Harford County.)

AMOS-HUGHES HOUSE. Built of granite and rubblestone, this home is a fine example of 19th-century Harford County masonry. Amos Hughes, son of John Hughes, built the house on a 100-acre tract purchased from his father. The date stone bears the inscription June 26, 1849. Records indicate that Amos Hughes lived here until his death in 1892. (Courtesy of Chris Weeks Collection, Historical Society of Harford County.)

STUMP-HARLAN HOUSE. In 1793, Henry Stump Sr. purchased 222 acres on Craig's Corner Road from his nephew John Stump, of Stafford. Although Henry had fours sons and one daughter, he left this property and his fishery on the Susquehanna River to only one of his sons, Reuben. Dr. David Harlan of Churchville, nephew of Reuben Stump, kept the property in the family until 1920. (Courtesy of Chris Weeks Collection, Historical Society of Harford County.)

STUMP-HOLLOWAY HOUSE. In 1800, William Stump, son of Henry Stump, contracted local stonemason David Hopkins to build this house for him on Stafford Road. William Stump died in 1831, and his widow sold the house to their son, Henry. Mrs. Stump continued to live there with her son until her death in 1869. Henry died in 1872 and left the farm to his nephews Albert and William Holloway. Their descendents still own the property today. (Courtesy of Chris Weeks Collection, Historical Society of Harford County.)

SEAMAN SMITH HOUSE. Charles Corman Smith, grandson of Thomas Smith, the ferry operator, built this house on Craig's Corner Road in 1860. The property still remains in privately ownership. (Courtesy of Chris Weeks Collection, Historical Society of Harford County.)

WORTHINGTON-MINNICK HOUSE. This stone house on Craig's Corner Road, also known as the Spencer House, was built in the mid-19th century by an "economically-minded" owner. The house was built of fieldstones taken from the surrounding fields. Although the stones are randomly placed and held together with inexpensive mortar, the house has withstood the test of time and remains a private residence. (Courtesy of Chris Weeks Collection, Historical Society of Harford County.)

FRIENDSHIP. John Cooley (1755–1809) and wife Sarah Anne Gilbert (1760–1832) lived in the stone section, built *c.* 1798, with their four slaves. In 1865, Stephen B. Hanna bought the property and added the two-story frame addition. (Courtesy of Chris Weeks Collection, Historical Society of Harford County.)

BOWMAN-STEARNS HOUSE. This log house was built *c.* 1850 on Rock Run Road in Level by cabinetmaker William S. Bowman. The property left the Bowman family in 1881. Annie Hughes Stearn and her husband, Leonard Stearn, lived here and raised 10 children. Leonard ran the store, and Annie devoted her life to two things: her family and her church. She was an active member of the Hopewell United Methodist Church as a devoted Sunday school teacher and loyal worker for nearly 80 years. (Courtesy of Chris Weeks Collection, Historical Society of Harford County.)

EDWARD WILKINSON FARM. Edward Wilkinson purchased this farm on Rock Run Road in Level in 1880. He hired John B. Bailey, local carpenter, wheelwright, and undertaker, to remodel the house on the property. Bailey added a touch of flair and fantasy to the house by adding turrets, fancy porches, and bay windows, novelties for the small community. (Courtesy of Chris Weeks Collection, Historical Society of Harford County.)

JEREMIAH SILVER HOUSE. In 1853, Jeremiah Silver built this house, also known as Lebanon, with plans designed by Mr. Reasin, from Aberdeen. Silver had a dairy operation involving five different farms in the county. He also served as an elder in the Presbyterian Church and was involved in local politics. The farm, now known as Seven Springs Farm, is owned by the Katharine and William Reese family. (Courtesy of Chris Weeks Collection, Historical Society of Harford County.)

Six

SUSQUEHANNA STATE PARK

The State of Maryland Department of Natural Resources purchased approximately 3,600 acres in the Rock Run–Lapidum area in 1958. This land includes the restored historic area consisting of the Rock Run Mansion (or Carter-Archer House), the Rock Run Mill, and the Jersey Tollhouse. The park offers many amenities for nature lovers, including a campground, picnic area, and boat launch facility on the Susquehanna. Deer Creek provides a haven for freshwater fishing, tubing, swimming, and canoeing. Long gone are the days of the thriving fishing industry along the river, although today one may still enjoy recreational fishing along its banks. The saltwater environment of the river offers catfish, herring, perch, rockfish, shad, and striped bass for anglers.

SUSQUEHANNA TRAIL. Miles of scenic hiking trails wind their way through the grounds of Susquehanna State Park. Some trails follow the old pathways of the Susquehannock tribe, the first settlers in this area. Others follow the dirt roads used long ago for travel to and from the banks of the Susquehanna. (Courtesy of David Duchon.)

Rock Run House, Front View. Due to the efforts of historic preservationists and the State of Maryland, the Rock Run House (also known as the Carter-Archer house) has been preserved. The home features antique furnishings from the 19th century. (Courtesy of David Duchon.)

Rock Run House, Back View. A view of the back of the house reveals its L-shaped design. The house has 13 rooms. In the basement, there is a wine cellar and an indoor smokehouse. In the large kitchen, there is a cooking hearth, where meals were prepared many years ago. (Courtesy of David Duchon.)

ROCK RUN MILL. This four-story stone building still has milling machinery inside. The water wheel weighs 12 tons and turned from the weight of the water. While in operation, the mill was a center of community activity when local farmers brought grain to be ground into meal. Now the restored Rock Run Mill offers corn-grinding demonstrations on weekends during the summer months. (Courtesy of David Duchon.)

MILL. This is another view of the Rock Run Mill, as seen looking from Stafford Road towards the Susquehanna River. (Courtesy of David Duchon.)

MILL RACE. The mill race was constructed for the purpose of channeling water into the mill. The flow of water from Rock Run Creek collects in a pond. From there, the water enters the race. (Courtesy of David Duchon.)

GATE AT THE MILL RACE. The water entering the mill race is controlled by a gate, like the one shown here. (Courtesy of David Duchon.)

MILLER'S HOUSE. This house provided living quarters for the men hired by the Stumps, Carters, and Archers to run Rock Run Mill. Its construction is credited to either John Stump of Stafford or John Carter of Rock Run. It also served as an inn for travelers on the road and canal. Now it serves as a residence for park personnel. (Courtesy of David Duchon.)

TOLL HOUSE. The Rock Run Bridge spanned the Susquehanna River from 1818 to 1854. A toll was charged for crossing the one-mile bridge, and the toll keeper lived here. Some of the tolls included: one score of sheep and hosts, 6¢; a score of cattle, 12¢; coach, stagecoach, or phaeton with two horses, 12¢, each additional horse 5¢. The fee for a wagon was based on the size of the wheels. The bridge was destroyed by ice in 1856 and never rebuilt. (Courtesy of David Duchon.)

CARRIAGE BARN. This two-story building was once a carriage barn for the estate at Rock Run during the 19th century. The lower section housed the carriages, and the upper level was used as a storage area. The carriage barn has recently been restored by the State Park. Near the barn is an outside bathroom, or "privy," which was used before indoor plumbing was available. This privy has accommodations for three people and was appropriately called a "three-holer." (Courtesy of David Duchon.)

SPRINGHOUSE. The springhouse was built between 1794 and 1804 to cover the source of drinking water used in the Rock Run House and Mill. It also served as a cool place to store milk, butter, and other foods to delay their spoiling. (Courtesy of David Duchon.)

WATERFALL. A beautiful waterfall in the park offers a tranquil spot for reflection. (Courtesy of David Duchon.)

STREAM. Picturesque streams like this can be found throughout the park. (Courtesy of David Duchon.)

BALD EAGLE. The park offers a habitat for the endangered bald eagle. Avid birdwatchers know the locations of their large nests. (Courtesy of David Duchon.)

DUCK. Wild ducks also enjoy the waters of Deer Creek and the Susquehanna River and make their home in Susquehanna State Park. The Susquehanna Flats at the head of the Chesapeake Bay were once a noted hunting ground for wild ducks and geese. Decoys carved by local residents have become collector's items, and some decoy carvers have received national and worldwide recognition for their work. (Courtesy of David Duchon.)

STONE WALLS. Dry stone walls such as these meander throughout the park property. Some are restored, but others are overgrown, barely visible, or in sad need of repair. The walls served as boundaries between landowners. (Courtesy of David Duchon.)

OLD ROAD. There are still visible signs of some of the old roadways through the park, especially those leading down to the riverfront. These roads played an important role in transporting goods to and from the riverfront. (Courtesy of David Duchon.)

THE END OF THE TRAIL. Approximately 12 miles of scenic hiking trails wind up and down through the park, connecting various points of interest. (Courtesy of David Duchon.)

Seven

STEPPINGSTONE MUSEUM

The Steppingstone Museum buildings are arranged in a rural setting. The c. 1771 stone farmhouse sits on a hill at the end of a quiet country lane. From the formal garden, surrounded by stone-fenced fields, one has a panoramic view of the Susquehanna River. Old restored farm tools occupy the implement sheds, and shops contain the tools of the blacksmith, woodworker, cooper, potter, wheelwright, dairy farmer, spinner, and weaver. In the big barn, there is an exhibit of a late-19th-century general store and a veterinarian's office. A carriage barn houses farm equipment, carriages, wagons, and sleighs. A replica of a late-19th-century canning house features artifacts from local Harford County canneries. The museum grounds are enhanced by a variety of trees, shrubs, perennial flowers, and an herb garden.

MUSEUM ENTRANCE SIGN. Set in the golden age of American agriculture, the Steppingstone Museum features the artifacts, arts, and crafts of the homes and farms of the 19th and early 20th centuries. Steppingstone is a not-for-profit museum dedicated to preserving and demonstrating the rural arts and crafts of the period from 1880 to 1920. (Courtesy of David Duchon.)

"STEPPINGSTONE." This slate slab was once located on the farm of museum founder J. Edmund "Ed" Bull. Prior to that, according to the inscription, it was located at the homes of his grandfather Jacob Bull and father Charles A. Bull. Ed Bull founded the museum in 1970, naming it "Steppingstone." A stepping-stone was used to step onto a carriage or a horse. After Bull's death in 1976, the museum was moved to its present location at Land of Promise on Quaker Bottom Road in Susquehanna State Park. (Courtesy of David Duchon.)

MUSEUM VISITOR'S CENTER. This farmhouse built, around 1940, was used as a residence for tenant farmers. It now serves as a visitor center and as office space for museum employees. (Courtesy of Steppingstone Museum Archives.)

J. EDMUND BULL. This early photograph shows Steppingstone Museum's founder when he worked as a banker in New York, before retiring to Harford County. He had decided on a career in finance rather than following in the footsteps of his grandfather Jacob Bull and father, Charles Bull, as architects and builders. (Courtesy of Steppingstone Museum Archives.)

ED BULL IN THE SHOPS. Founder Ed Bull is shown here in one of the shops of the museum. The sleigh is called a "courting sleigh." (Courtesy of Steppingstone Museum Archives.)

THE FOARD BLACKSMITH SHOP. This shop, once located in Level, was moved to the museum complex in 1983. Volunteer blacksmiths demonstrate the skills of their trade here for tours and on weekends during the museum season. (Courtesy of David Duchon.)

THE FOARD BLACKSMITH SHOP. This photograph shows the interior of the blacksmith shop. A wax replica of Bill Foard greets visitors. (Courtesy of Joe Cambria.)

GILES-PAUL FARMHOUSE. The two-story section of the stone farmhouse is believed to have been built by Nathaniel Giles, a Quaker and prosperous merchant. His wife and their five children lived here. The middle section and frame kitchen on the end were added by John Gilman Paul, a wealthy bachelor from Baltimore who purchased the property from the Macklem sisters in 1940. (Courtesy of David Duchon.)

THE FARMHOUSE C. 1939. John Gilman Paul is credited with extensive renovations to the house. The frame section was torn down, and he added a middle section in stone and a frame kitchen on the end. (Courtesy of the Historical Society of Harford County.)

114

VIEW FROM THE COURTYARD. The trees have slowly taken away the house's view of the river. (Courtesy Steppingstone Museum Archives.)

VIEW FROM THE COURTYARD C. 1939. This photograph shows the view from the farmhouse yard to the Susquehanna River at the time Paul purchased the property. (Courtesy of the Historical Society of Harford County.)

PARLOR. This is the formal sitting room of the farmhouse, with an empire sofa, rocking chair, pump organ, and other antique furnishings. (Courtesy of Joe Cambria.)

PUMP ORGAN. The pump organ was once in the Darlington United Methodist Church. It was donated to the museum by Lilma Huntley, church member and museum volunteer, when the church decided to buy a new one. Mrs. Huntley plays the organ on special-event weekends there. (Courtesy of Joe Cambria.)

SEWING ROOM. This room displays an old Singer sewing machine and numerous frames of prizewinning lace exhibits. (Courtesy of Joe Cambria.)

KITCHEN. The kitchen is representative of the late 19th century, with its wood-burning stove, dry sink, and ice box. (Courtesy of Joe Cambria.)

Master Bedroom. A dresser in the master bedroom shows hair implements, a mirror, gloves, and other common accessories of the time. (Courtesy of Joe Cambria.)

Children's Bedroom. The children's room contains a wonderful array of toys from the late 19th and early 20th centuries. A variety of dolls, games, and books adorns the room. (Courtesy of Joe Cambria.)

BARN. This old barn is no longer home to cattle and other farm animals. It now houses the general store and other museum exhibits. The spinning and weaving room and the decoy carver's shop are also located here. (Courtesy of Joe Cambria.)

COW. This weather vane in the shape of a cow sits on top of the Steppingstone Barn. (Courtesy of David Duchon.)

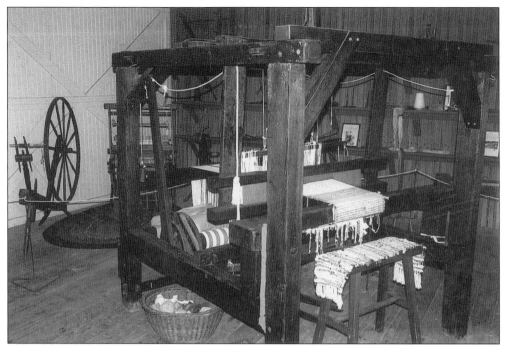

SPINNING AND WEAVING ROOM. This room contains many different sizes of looms: an inkle loom, lap loom, and belt loom. The large floor loom dates to the early 19th century. Weaving on looms created necessities like rugs, blankets, and linens. (Courtesy of Joe Cambria.)

SPINNING AND WEAVING ROOM. There is an extensive collection of spinning wheels in this exhibit. The constant spinning of the wheel, either by hand or foot, spins the wool into yarn to be used for knitting or weaving. (Courtesy of Joe Cambria.)

WOODWORKING SHOP. The array of tools in this exhibit was used for felling trees for wood to be used in building houses or making furniture, windows, doors, and fancy trimwork. The museum has an extensive collection of hand planes and a foot-powered lathe and jigsaw. (Courtesy of Joe Cambria.)

COOPER SHOP. The cooper was an important craftsman during his time, primarily making shipping barrels, buckets, and wash tubs. (Courtesy of Joe Cambria.)

DAIRY SHOP. The dairy shop exhibits implements used for milking cows and churning butter. There are a variety of churns on display here (Courtesy of Joe Cambria.)

FARM AND GARDEN TOOL SHOP. This shop has an assortment of small tools used in farming the land, including rakes, hoes, shovels, grain cradles, hay knives, and hay forks. (Courtesy of Joe Cambria.)

POTTER'S SHED. This was originally a fish drying building. Gilman Paul had it disassembled and, with some modifications, rebuilt on the property at Steppingstone. It is now used by the museum's potters, who demonstrate their craft during the season. (Courtesy of Steppingstone Museum Archives.)

WHEELWRIGHT SHOP. A wheelwright/blacksmith made wheels for wagons, carriages, and buggies. (Courtesy of Steppingstone Museum Archives.)

CORN CRIB. This building was used for air-drying corn. The raised structure allowed for the flow of air in the drying process and also evidently prevented the rodent population from gaining access to the corn. (Courtesy of Steppingstone Museum Archives.)

CANNING HOUSE. Although the building is a replica of a tomato canning house, it contains authentic equipment used in the processing of tomatoes. The canning industry was in its heyday in Harford County during the late 19th century and into the first part of the 20th. (Courtesy of David Duchon.)

EARLY TRANSPORTATION. The museum has a collection of antique carriages, wagons, carts, sleighs, and farm equipment. (Courtesy of Steppingstone Museum Archives.)

1914 INTERNATIONAL TRACTOR. Antique farm equipment, such as this 1914 tractor, is featured in the museum's exhibits. (Courtesy of Joe Cambria.)

STONE WALLS. These stone walls surround the property at Steppingstone Museum. Some were presumably built with slave labor during the 19th century. (Courtesy of Steppingstone Museum Archives.)

HERB GARDEN. The herb garden features cooking, medicinal, and tea herbs. In the center is a sundial. (Courtesy of Steppingstone Museum Archives.)

BIBLIOGRAPHY

The Harford County Directory. Baltimore: State Directories Publishing Company, 1953.

The Land of Promise at the Steppingstone Museum. Steppingstone House Committee: 1982.

Park, John. *Maryland Mining Heritage Guide*. South Miami: Stonerose Publishing Company, 2002.

"The Rural Arts and Crafts of Harford County and the Steppingstone Museum." *Harford Historical Bulletin*. Historical Society of Harford County: 1996.

Weeks, Chris. *An Architectural History of Harford County, Maryland*. Baltimore: Johns Hopkins University Press, 1996.

Wright, C. Milton. *Harford Heritage*. Glen Burnie, MD: French-Bray Printing Company, 1967.

Interviews were conducted with the following:

Josephine and Bernie Bodt
Elma Bowman
Nelson Bowman
Pat and Art Elsner
Robert Janssen, historian, Level Volunteer Fire Station
Johnny Johnson, Arundel Corporation
Mary Macklem Peal
Richard Sherrill, head of archives, Historical Society of Harford County
Mary and Nelson Slye
Isabelle Stearn
Rebecca and Scott Walker

UNCOMFORTABLY
HAPPILY

YEON-SIK HONG

Translated by Hellen Jo

Drawn & Quarterly

drawnandquarterly.com

First English edition: May 2017
Printed in China
10 9 8 7 6 5 4 3 2 1

Library and Archives Canada Cataloguing in Publication
Hong, Yeon-sik
[*Bul-pyeon-ha-go haeng-bo-ka-ge*. English]
  Uncomfortably Happily / Yeon-sik Hong; translated by Hellen Jo.

Translation of: *Bul-pyeon-ha-go haeng-bo-ka-ge*.
ISBN 978-1-77046-260-1 (paperback)

1. Hong, Yeon-sik—Comic books, strips, etc. 2. Cartoonists—Korea
(South)—Biography—Comic books, strips, etc. 3. Country life—Korea (South)—
Comic books, strips, etc. 4. Solitude—Korea (South)—Comic books, strips,
etc. 5. Graphic novels. I. Jo, Hellen, translator II. Title. III. Title:
Bul-pyeon-ha-go haeng-bo-ka-ge. English.

NC1729.H65A2 2017   741.5'9519   C2016-904133-6

Published in the USA by Drawn & Quarterly,
a client publisher of Farrar, Straus and Giroux
Orders: 888.330.8477

Published in Canada by Drawn & Quarterly,
a client publisher of Raincoast Books
Orders: 800.663.5714

Published in the United Kingdom by Drawn & Quarterly,
a client publisher of Publishers Group UK
Orders: info@pguk.co.uk

Late Summer

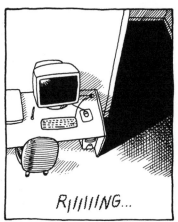

9

LABEL: TASTY OTTOGI CURRY

10

· · ·

THE MANU-
SCRIPT? NO.
I'LL POST IT
BY NOON.

ALSO, DID
YOU BY ANY
CHANCE CALL
ME AT EIGHT
O'CLOCK THIS
MORNING?

IN THE FUTURE, EVEN IF THE
MANUSCRIPT IS LATE, DON'T
CALL BEFORE NINE.

WE WON'T
PICK UP!

THAT CALL EARLIER
WAS FROM YOUR
PUBLISHER?

IT'S
CRAZY!

MAKING
MANUSCRIPT
DEMANDS AT
8:00 A.M....

MMF
MMF

THAT'S
A LITTLE
MUCH.

NOM
NOM

KRNTCH
KRNTCH

· · ·

DAMN
IT.

*REFERS TO THE PARK CHAN-WOOK THRILLER, OLDBOY.

YOU MUST BE TIRED OF HOUSE HUNTING ALONE, HUH?

......

THERE ARE SO MANY HOUSES OUT THERE. I CAN'T BELIEVE HOW HARD IT IS TO FIND ONE FOR US.

WE'LL FIND ONE. IT'LL JUST TAKE TIME.

DID YOU GET A LOT OF WORK DONE?

HERE AND THERE...

THE TRAFFIC IS SO NOISY. IT'S HARD TO FOCUS.

WELL, OUR APARTMENT'S ON LOAN FROM YOUR OLD PUBLISHER...

AND SINCE THAT PROJECT HAS FIZZLED OUT, IT MAKES SENSE TO FIND A NEW, QUIET HOME!

IF WE REALLY WANT TO LEAVE THIS PLACE, I SHOULD COME HELP YOU LOOK.

WHAT DO YOU THINK ABOUT GYEONGGI-DO, NEAR SEOUL?

OH, THAT COULD BE GOOD!

◇ CLAP

THE AIR QUALITY'S GOTTA BE BETTER THERE!

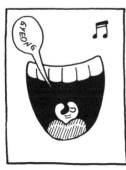

WELCOME TO GYEONGGI-DO... ♫

WHERE NATURE AND PEOPLE LIVE IN PERFECT HARMONY...

COME EXPERIENCE LEISURELY COUNTRY LIVING...

IS THERE REALLY ANY NEED TO LIVE IN SEOUL?

IS THERE?

ONLY THIRTY MINUTES FROM SEOUL...

THE AIR IS CLEAR AND THE CITY IS QUIET...

AND BECAUSE IT'S STILL UNDER MARKET PRICE...

SIGN: WELCOME TO GYEONGGI-DO

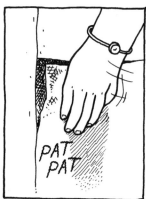

PAT
PAT

THERE AREN'T MANY LEASES AVAILABLE THESE DAYS.

IT'S NOT EVEN THAT MUCH CHEAPER THAN SEOUL...

FSHHHH

SLIDE

BUT THE AIR QUALITY IS BETTER, AND THE VIEWS TOO. YOU CAN SEE THE MOUNTAINS...

WHAT MOUNTAIN IS THAT WAAAAY OVER THERE?

...YOU'D LIKE TO DRAW IN A QUIET LOCATION? WELL, WHY DIDN'T YOU SAY SO SOONER?

THERE'S NO OTHER PLACE LIKE THIS. ONCE YOU SEE IT, YOU'LL UNDERSTAND.

THE LONG DRIVE MIGHT BE A DRAG.

SMELL THAT CLEAN AIR!

SKREE

····· ····· ·····
·· ···· ····
···
···· ···· ····
···· ····

IT'S GOT A GARDEN AND A YARD, BUT THE HOUSE IS SO RUN-DOWN!

CHEONG-PYEONG IS JUST WAY TOO FAR!

THE HOUSE IS GREAT, BUT DO WE REALLY WANT TO LIVE IN THE SAME BUILDING AS THE OWNER?

AND WHAT'S WITH THE HIGH RENT? IT'S NOT EVEN MUCH CHEAPER THAN SEOUL...

WHAT DO WE DO?

YOU'VE BEEN TOO DISTRACTED LOOKING FOR HOUSES TO DO ANY WORK, HAVEN'T YOU, HONEY?

I'LL RESEARCH MORE LISTINGS. YOU CATCH UP ON YOUR COMICS.

IT'S NOT THE HOUSING PRICES THAT HAVE GONE CRAZY— IT'S THIS BASTARD OF A COUNTRY.

ALL THE PEOPLE WHO OWN HOMES HAVE GONE CRAZY TOO.

?

HONK

VROOM

BEEP BEEP

HONK HONK

HONK

HONK
VROOM
BEEP

WOW, YOU'RE UP EARLY!

WASH UP QUICKLY!

YAWWHN

IT'S IN POCHEON, BUT ON THE MAP IT'S CLOSE TO NAM-YANGJU.

...BUT IT'S STILL FAR FROM SEOUL, RIGHT?

THERE'S A STAND-ALONE HOUSE, AND A BIG GARDEN. THEY SAY IT'S QUIET BECAUSE IT'S SURROUNDED BY MOUNTAINS.

광릉내터미널

청량리 ↔ 광릉

사무실

LET'S SEE... THE NEXT BUS ARRIVES AT...!

THAT'S NOT FOR AN HOUR AND A HALF!!

YES, WE'VE ARRIVED AT GWANGNEUNG TERMINAL.

배차시간표

HONEY, THEY SAY A TAXI WOULD BE FASTEST.

THE OAK TREE REST AREA?

VROOM

23

24

LOOK HOW CLEAR THAT STREAM IS!

PSH, IT'S WAY TOO CLEAR FOR THERE TO BE ANY FISH.

WE'RE GOING ON A PROPER WALK!

YEAH!

INHALE

HAAA

THE AIR IS SO FRESH!

30

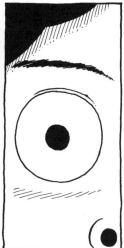

SIGN: GOODBYE SEOUL CITY LIMITS

33

OR IF I'M JUST RUNNING AWAY BECAUSE I CAN'T HANDLE CITY LIFE...

VROOM

JUST FOLLOW THE ROAD STRAIGHT UP THE MOUNTAIN.

VROOOOOOM

KA-CHUNK

Fall Part 1

WE NEED TO UNPACK. ARE YOU JUST GONNA LIE AROUND LIKE THAT?

YAWN

THINKING ABOUT THE BOTH OF US HERE, ALONE ON THE MOUNTAIN...IT FEELS WEIRD, DOESN'T IT?

WE HAVE TO UNPACK SO WE CAN GET TO WORK.

ALL RIGHT.

I GET IT.

CLEAN THAT UP!

AND THAT TOO!

HNG

MEOOOOW

PANT PANT

GO AWAY. WHY DO YOU GET TO LOAF AROUND ALL DAY?

PURRR PURRR

IT'S JUST A FEW LEAVES... WILL IT SURVIVE?

HOW FAR ARE WE GOING?

LET'S JUST WALK TO THAT POINT OVER THERE.

HAS IT BEEN RAINING A LOT? THE RIVER'S HIGH.

WOW, WHO KNEW...

IT'S SO PRETTY!

SHF

SWISH

...WE MUST BE THE ONLY ONES ON THIS MOUNTAIN.

HONEY, WHAT ARE YOU DO-ING?

TOO BAD THE SKY ISN'T CLEARER. WE'D BE ABLE TO SEE SO MANY STARS...

WAIT!

KWOHHHHHH

WHAT...WHAT IS THAT?

KWOHHHHH

KWOHHHHH

KWOHHHHHH

I KNOW ROE DEER PRETTY WELL, AND THAT'S DEFINITELY THE SOUND OF A ROE DEER.

KWOHHHHH

LATER I LEARNED IT WAS JUST A PHEASANT.

HELLO?

YEAH, THE MOUNTAIN WE MOVED TO HAS WEAK RECEPTION, SO...

....

DISCONNECTED AGAIN!

YAWN

TOMORROW IS SUNDAY.

THEY CAN INSTALL THE INTERNET AND PHONE LINE ON MONDAY, RIGHT?

I REALLY CAN'T GET MUCH WORK DONE WITHOUT THE INTERNET.

...WHEN WILL WE HAVE TIME TO CLEAN UP THE FIELD?

WE'VE COME TOO DEEP INTO THE FOREST. WE CAN'T USE OUR CELL PHONES AT ALL.

JUST USE THE LANDLINE.

CLATTER
CLATTER

종량제
봉투
내흥면

종량제
봉투
내흥면

....

HONEY, WHEN'S YOUR NEXT PAYCHECK COMING IN?

CLATTER
CLATTER

IF I SETTLE THE CONTRACT TOMORROW... MAYBE NEXT MONTH?

WE HAVE A LOT OF EXPENSES TO TAKE CARE OF.

HMM...

IF WE'RE CAREFUL, WE SHOULD BE OKAY. IT'S NOT LIKE WE'RE IN THE CITY WHERE THERE'S LOTS TO SPEND MONEY ON.

. . .

WE SHOULDN'T BE RENTING; I'D LOVE TO BUILD OUR OWN HOUSE IN A PLACE LIKE THIS.

ONE DAY.

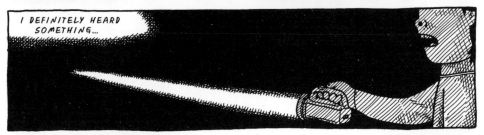

THAT TOOK TWENTY-FIVE MINUTES.

HELLO! DOES THE BUS TO CHEONGNYANGNI STOP HERE?

JUST LEFT!

PLOP

MUMBLE MUMBLE

DO THESE DAMN HICK BUSES ALWAYS LEAVE AHEAD OF SCHEDULE?

SHIT...I'M GONNA NEED A CAR!

HYUNRI NAECHON CHEONGNYANGNI

NOD

NOD

SCREECH

청량리행

11

STOP! HALT!

청량리 — 내촌

11

THESE COUNTRY BUSES HAVE NO CONCEPT OF TIME, AND THAT'S IF THEY EVEN SHOW UP.

₩8,500,000!*

HOW CAN THE MANUSCRIPT FEE KEEP GETTING SMALLER?

WE'RE PAYING YOU ABOVE THE STANDARD RATE, MR. HONG.

AND OUR SITUATION IS A BIT...

SURE, IT'S FOR ONE PAPERBACK VOLUME, BUT ₩8,500,000...

*ROUGHLY $8,000 U.S.

HOW LONG DO I HAVE TO KEEP DOING THIS KIND OF WORK?

DING

. . . .

SQUEAK

I'M COMPROMISING MY ART TO EARN A LIVING. I HAVE TO SURVIVE SOMEHOW.

CRINKLE

FOR TEN THOUSAND COPIES OF THE PAPERBACK, THE ONGOING RATE OF ROY-ALTIES IS 6 PERCENT. IN THE EVENT THAT THE PRINT RUN SELLS OUT, THE BOOK CONTRACT GUARANTEES ₩8,500,000.

I SUPPOSE THAT LOOKS MORE RESPECTABLE THAN "INTELLECTUAL PROPERTY WAIVER."

WHIRRR...

저작재산권 양도계약서

WELL, LET'S NOT DO ANY MORE WORK THAN THEY'RE PAYING US FOR.

WHIRRR

PAPER: INTELLECTUAL PROPERTY CONTRACT

47

HEY NOW, HOW ARE YOU EVER GOING TO MAKE ANY MONEY LIKE THAT?

I'M JUST SAYING, YOU SHOULD HIRE LOTS OF ASSISTANTS AND OPERATE A FACTORY SYSTEM.

ARE YOU KIDDING ME? YOU THINK MANAGING ASSISTANTS IS EASY?

WHIRR...

BUT I KNOW THE TRUTH: THE DAY EARNING A LIVING COMPLETELY OVERTAKES MY ABILITY TO MAKE MY OWN ART IS THE DAY MY WRISTS WILL BREAK AND I WON'T BE ABLE TO WRITE OR DRAW ANYMORE.

WHIRR...

MY ORIGINAL PLAN WAS TO EARN A LOT OF ROYALTIES DURING THIS LEAVE OF ABSENCE, AND THEN AFTER RETURNING TO SCHOOL, DEVOTE MYSELF COMPLETELY TO MY OWN CREATIVE WORK.

...I WAS NAÏVE.

WORK IS SLOW AND LIFE IS HARD ENOUGH...AND TODAY I'VE HAD TO SIGN YET ANOTHER CONTRACT...

PEDESTAL: FOUNDER

IT'S A REAL VICIOUS CIRCLE!

HEY, YOU!

TIRED, HUH? WALKIN' OUT TO THE BUS, THEN BACK HOME ON THE SUBWAY...THE WHOLE DAY'S BEEN SHOT.

...

WHY DON'T YOU OPEN THAT WINDOW? NOW THAT YOU'VE DITCHED TOEGYEWON, THE AIR WILL BE NICE.

EASY FOR YOU TO SAY.

WHERE ARE YOU, HONEY?

I'M GETTING OFF THE BUS NOW.

SCREECH

YOU SHOULD TAKE A TAXI HOME.

A TAXI WON'T GO UP THE MOUNTAIN...

SO I'LL JUST WALK.

TAKE A TAXI!

내촌택시

내촌식당

TAXI

49

SONG: "SOMEHOW, AS I BEHOLD YOU" (1982) BY KOREAN ROCK GROUP, SONGOLMAE

H...HONEY?!

IT FELT LIKE SOMEONE MIGHT SUDDENLY GRAB ME FROM BEHIND, SO I RAN DOWNHILL LIKE CRAZY, BUT THEN I COULDN'T STOP MYSELF.

HAH

HAH

HAH

WHY DID YOU COME OUT? IT'S DARK. YOU SHOULD HAVE STAYED INSIDE.

YOU SCARED ME.

DID THE CONTRACT MEETING GO WELL?

YEAH, LET'S TALK ABOUT IT INSIDE.

51

WE HAVE TO GET GROCERIES TOMORROW. WE'RE ALMOST OUT OF THE NECESSI-TIES...

ALL RIGHT. TOMORROW'S THE FARMERS' MARKET, ISN'T IT?

ANYTHING INTEREST-ING HAPPEN TODAY?

CLICK

A BUNCH OF HIKERS PARKED THEIR CARS AGAINST THE RETAINING WALL.

UGH.

· · · ·

WHEN YOU'RE HOME ALONE, LOCK THE DOOR, OKAY?

OKAY...

THUD

52

YES, I'M NEARLY FINISHED...

I'LL HAVE IT DONE BY FIVE O'CLOCK.

TOMORROW IS SATURDAY. IF YOU DON'T GET IT IN TODAY, WE WON'T HAVE IT UNTIL MONDAY.

YOU HAVE TO GET IT IN TODAY!

I'LL TURN IT IN ON TIME. GO ABOUT YOUR DAY...

ALSO, THERE ARE REVISIONS FOR THE PREVIOUS SECTION THAT I NEED TO GO OVER WITH YOU—YOU'RE NOT IN A HURRY, ARE YOU?

WHY DOES IT HAVE TO BE OVER THE PHONE? LET'S CHAT ON INSTANT MESSENGER; MY EARS ARE HURTING...

OR SEND ME AN EMAIL.

BUT WHY?!

MY DINNER'S READY!

IT'LL TAKE JUST TWENTY, NO, TEN MINUTES! IT WON'T TAKE A MINUTE...

ARE YOU KIDDING ME? LAST TIME YOU SAID THAT, YOU KEPT ME TIED TO THE PHONE UNTIL MY FOOD GOT COLD!

SO, THE SECTIONS THAT NEED WORK...

HERE...

...AND HERE.

CALM DOWN, HONEY.

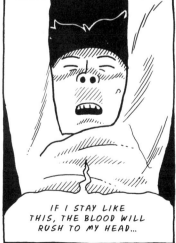

HEY!

THAT'S A BIT OF AN OVERREACTION, ISN'T IT?

THIS IS PRIVATE PROPERTY. YOU CAN'T PARK HERE.

THERE'S ROOM OVER ON THE SHOULDER.

WE WON'T BE HERE LONG. YOU'RE NOT EVEN USING THIS SPACE...

JUST LET US PARK.

SOME WELCOME!

THAT'S NOT THE POINT. THIS IS MY LAND. THAT ALONE IS REASON ENOUGH TO STOP YOU FROM PARKING HERE. I'D LIKE IT IF YOU MOVED YOUR CARS, NOW.

TSK, HE'LL GET INTO ANOTHER FIGHT.

YOU'D JUST END UP IN AN UNNECESSARY ARGUMENT.

.....

IF THEY DON'T RESPECT US, WHY SHOULD WE RESPECT THEM?

LET'S DEAL WITH IT IF IT HAPPENS AGAIN!

OKAY?

CHEST-NUTS!

THERE'S MORE UP THERE.

HERE'S ANOTH-ER!

ANOTH-ER!

FIRST WE NEED A SHOVEL AND A PICKAX. WE'LL BUY WHATEVER ELSE WE NEED LATER.

AND RUBBER BOOTS TO WEAR WHILE WE WORK!

CRUNCH

CRUNCH

IT REALLY SEEMS LIKE WE'RE LIVING SEPARATELY FROM THE REST OF THE NEIGHBORHOOD, DOESN'T IT?

WELL, WE ARE!

SEEMS READY FOR HARVEST.

ALREADY?

YEAH. LOOK HOW THE RICE BENDS UNDER ITS OWN WEIGHT.

HELLO.

AND WHO ARE YOU?

WE JUST MOVED INTO THAT HOUSE ON THE MOUNTAIN.

OH YEAH?

BEEN SO LONG SINCE I'VE GONE UP THAT WAY...

THERE'S A HOUSE UP THERE, EH?

YES, MA'AM!

YOU DON'T SAY! WELL, DON'T LET ME STOP YA—

YOU SAW IT TOO, RIGHT? SHE HAD A CIGARETTE IN EACH HAND.

WOOF WOOF

BARK BARK

WOOF WOOF

YOU'RE SAY-ING YOU LIVE WAY UP ON THAT THERE MOUNTAIN?!

참나무 휴게소

담배

BUT ISN'T LIVING UP ON THE MOUNTAIN SCARY?

COOL COLA COOL

...OH, WELL, HMM, NOT REALLY.

SIGN: OAK TREE REST AREA

59

LIVING UP THERE SEEMS MIGHTY SCARY TO ME...

I WANT A SODA!

Y'ALL SIBLINGS?

SIBLINGS?!

HO HO HO HO HO—OR NOT! HOW DO Y'ALL LOOK SO MUCH ALIKE?

GOODBYE!

COME AGAIN, HO HO HO!

YOU MUST BE PLEASED, DEAR. SHE SAID YOU LOOK LIKE ME.

NOT REALLY.

SLURRRP

...HONEY.

I DO FEEL A BIT SCARED WHEN I'M HOME ALONE... I THINK IT'D BE A GOOD IDEA TO GET A DOG.

I'VE HEARD THAT JINDOS MAKE GOOD GUARD DOGS, SO LET'S LOOK INTO IT. I'VE BEEN THINKING ABOUT IT ANYWAY...ALSO...

WHEN DO YOU THINK WE'LL GET A CAR?

A CAR? IN OUR SITUATION? WE'RE STILL IN DEBT!

60

I'M NOT SAYING LET'S GET ONE RIGHT NOW, BUT YOU CAN'T ARGUE THAT WE DON'T NEED ONE.

WHY DO WE NEED A CAR? THERE'S A BUS THAT GOES TO SEOUL!

DOES THE BUS EVER SHOW UP ON TIME? PLUS THERE AREN'T MANY ROUTES, AND IF YOU MISS ONE, YOU GOTTA TAKE A CAB...WHEW...

I CALCULATED IT, AND THE COST OF OWNING A CAR ISN'T ALL THAT DIFFERENT FROM THE COST OF PUBLIC TRANSPORTA-TION. AND WHAT ABOUT ALL THAT TIME WASTED WAITING FOR THE COUNTRY BUS?!

WHEN DID YOU FIGURE ALL THAT OUT?

EVEN IF WE HAVE TO WAIT A WHILE, LET'S GET ONE. IT'S NOT LIKE THERE ARE TRAIN TRACKS LAID ACROSS KOREA LIKE IN JAPAN. YOU NEED A CAR IN THE BOONIES!

WE SURE BOUGHT A LOT.

A PICK AND A HOE. AND WE NEEDED A NEW SICKLE ANY-WAY, SO IT WAS A GOOD PURCHASE.

VROOM

WE'RE HERE.

SKREE

YOU CAN'T GO UP THE HILL?

...AND SCRATCH THE UNDER-SIDE OF MY CAR?

THAT WAS RUDE.

BEFORE THE FALL RAIN COMES, LET'S TACKLE THE WEEDS AROUND THE HOUSE.

FMP

WHAT ARE YOU DOING?

WE'VE BOTH BEEN HOARDING BOOKS FOR YEARS THAT WE'LL NEVER READ AGAIN. GO GRAB SOME OF YOURS!

...

BEFORE WE CAN GROW A GARDEN,
WE HAVE TO CLEAR OUT THESE
PILES OF GARBAGE THAT HAVE
BEEN AROUND FOR WHO KNOWS
HOW MANY YEARS...

SAME WITH THE WEEDS IN
THE FRONT YARD...

LOOKING AROUND THE PROPERTY,
THERE ARE SO MANY THINGS
THAT NEED TO BE DONE...

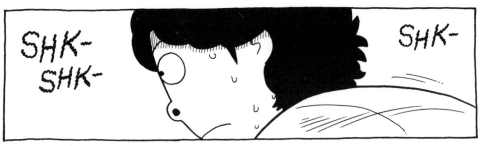

SHK-
SHK-

SHK-

SHK-

SHK-

SHK-

SHK-

SHK-

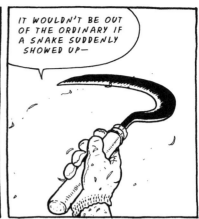

IT WOULDN'T BE OUT OF THE ORDINARY IF A SNAKE SUDDENLY SHOWED UP—

HISS

AHHH! YOU SCARED ME! WHAT, YOU SHOW UP BECAUSE I SAID SO?!

HONEY, WHAT ABOUT THIS?

VOILA!

HOWZIT LOOK?

YOU LOOK UNMISTAK-ABLY LIKE A VILLAGE YOUTH!

NO, WAIT— A VILLAGE OLD MAN!

I SHOULDN'T HAVE ASKED!

BUT YOUR SICKLE SKILLS ARE NOTHING TO SNEEZE AT!

THAT'S BECAUSE I TRIED IT EVERY TIME I VISITED MY UNCLE'S HOUSE IN THE COUNTRY.

WHEW! I'M NOT GOING TO BE ABLE TO CLEAR ALL THIS IN ONE DAY!

HERE, WATER.

AH!

GLUG GLUG

KYAAAAAH THAT'S REFRESHING!!

LET'S WASH UP AND EAT.

SOUNDS GOOD.

VROOM
VROOOOOOOOOOM
VVVROOM
VROOOOOOM

WHAT'S THIS?
YOU MADE A MEAL
ALL BY YOURSELF?

I DON'T
KNOW WHAT
YOU MEAN.

AHEM,
LET'S GIVE
IT A TASTE.

YUM, TASTES
GREAT!

EVERYTHING TASTES
BETTER WHEN YOU'RE
HUNGRY!

IF YOU
DON'T
HAVE
ANYTHING
NICE TO
SAY...

OH MY GOSH!

FLINCH

WHAT'S
WRONG?

CAN YOU
PLEASE...

SHF

TOSS

Fall Part 2

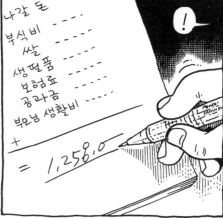

NOTE: EXPENSES—GROCERIES, NECESSITIES, INSURANCE, LIVING EXPENSES FOR PARENTS

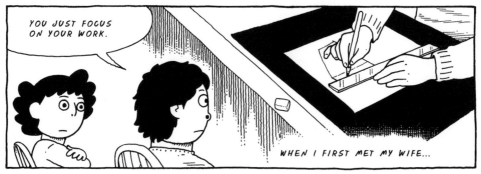

YOU JUST FOCUS ON YOUR WORK.

WHEN I FIRST MET MY WIFE...

SHE WANTED TO WORK AT AN ANIMATION STUDIO.

TEACH-ER!

EVENTUALLY, I WOULD LIKE TO BECOME A SHORT ANIMATION DIRECTOR.

IN THAT CASE...

YOU SHOULD PROBABLY ENROLL IN A MORE PROFESSIONAL PROGRAM AT ANOTHER SCHOOL. YOU MIGHT EVEN BE ABLE TO TRAIN ON THE JOB...

WHAT?!

OUR FOCUS HERE IS ON A COMICS CURRICULUM.

OH...I SEE...

BUT...

SINCE DRAWING IS A FOUNDATIONAL SKILL, CAN I STAY IN THIS CLASS WHILE I THINK ABOUT IT?

OF COURSE.

IF MY WIFE HAD LISTENED TO MY ADVICE BACK THEN...WOULD WE HAVE BECOME A COUPLE?

STILL WORKS.

SQUEAK

SQUEAK

. . . . .

SLOW DOWN. YOU SAID YOU'VE BEEN FALLING BEHIND ON WORK.

YOU'RE RIGHT.

WHEN YOU VISIT SOME VILLAGES, YOU THINK, "THIS IS A DYING NEIGHBORHOOD..." BUT HERE, THE SCENT OF GRAPES SEEMS TO GIVE THE WHOLE AREA A GOOD OLD DOSE OF VITALITY.

HELLO!

HELLO...

WE MOVED INTO THE HOUSE BELOW YOURS EARLIER THIS FALL.

OH, ZAT SO?

THAT GENTLEMAN THERE LIVES HERE. I'M JUST A FRIEND.

I COME DOWN FROM SEOUL OFTEN.

OH, YOU DO?

THEY SEEM TO VISIT ONCE OR TWICE A MONTH. THEY LIVE IN SEOUL.

I THOUGHT IT WAS A VACANT PROPERTY, BUT HONESTLY, I'M RELIEVED TO HAVE A NEIGHBOR WE CAN CHAT WITH ONCE IN A WHILE.

HONEY, COME TAKE A LOOK AT THIS.

YOU DON'T THINK THE PIG'S EYES LOOK TOO BLACK AND BEADY ON HIS FACE, DO YOU?

WHY? I LIKE IT.

COMPARED TO THE REST OF HIS FACE, THE EYES LOOK LIKE BULGING BLACK BEANS, AND IT'S A BIT UNPLEASANT...

BRRRRING

THIS IS IT!

YOU HAVEN'T PAID THE COLOR ASSISTANT YET, HAVE YOU?

NO.

LET'S SETTLE THE NEXT VOLUME'S CONTRACT QUICKLY THEN. THERE'S NO CHOICE BUT TO PAY THIS VOLUME'S COLOR FEE WITH THAT CONTRACT MONEY.

BUT THAT CONTRACT MONEY IS FOR NEXT MONTH'S LIVING EXPENSES...

SURE, THE PUBLISHER CAN HIRE A PART-TIME COLORIST, BUT THEN THE COLOR FEE HAS TO COME OUT OF MY ROYALTIES.

GOING CRAZY...

THIS IS WHY YOU NEED TO WORK MORE QUICKLY AND MOVE ON.

IF YOU FALL BEHIND, YOU'LL ONLY SUFFER.

AND OVER NOTHING ...

FROM THE INITIAL ROYALTIES OF ₩5,000,000, ₩2,000,000 GOES TO COLOR, YOU TAKE OUT ₩1,000,000 FOR INKING, AND THERE'S ₩2,000,000 LEFT...

IF ONE VOLUME TAKES THREE...NO, FOUR MONTHS TO FINISH, THEN HOW THE HELL...

I JUST DON'T HAVE THE CONFI- DENCE TO PUSH MY WAY OUT...

WHAT THE HELL DO THEY EXPECT US TO LIVE ON?

HONEY, INSTEAD OF DOING THIS, LET'S GO OUT AND GET SOME AIR, OKAY?

HMM?

WITH THIS MOUNTAIN BEING THE LOWER EDGE OF THE GWANGNEUNG ARBORETUM...

YEAH.

OW, THAT STINGS!

DO YOU THINK IT'S TOO MUCH OF A LUXURY FOR JUST THE TWO OF US TO BE ABLE TO ENJOY ALL THIS BEAUTIFUL SCENERY AND CLEAN AIR...?

IS THERE A HOLE IN MY SHOE?

ANOTHER PAYCHECK WILL COME IN FROM SOMEWHERE, AND WE'LL MAKE OUR LIVING EXPENSES NEXT MONTH, SOMEHOW. DON'T WORRY ABOUT IT TOO MUCH.

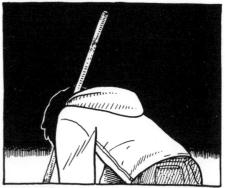

HOO - HOOOT

HOOOOOOOT

AN AVERAGE OF ₩800,000 PER MONTH... I'M SO EXHAUSTED.

HONEY...

...ARE YOU SLEEPING?

NO...

IS THAT A BIRD CALL?

MUST BE, RIGHT?

CAN'T YOU SLEEP?

...NO.

THIS PROJECT I'M WORKING ON, I'M ALREADY ON THE SECOND VOLUME...

SAY THEY WANTED ME TO DRAW THREE STARS IN THE PUPILS, OR THEY REQUESTED I CHANGE THE COMIC IN SOME OTHER CHILDISH WAY—I'D FIX IT THE WAY THEY WANTED.

THEN I WOULD HYPNOTIZE MYSELF.

THIS IS YOUR JOOOOOOOB...FOR MONEYYYYY...

IF YOU HIT THE JACKPOT, YOU'LL BE HIT BY THE ROYALTIES LIGHT-NING BOLT...

SCRITCH SCRATCH SCRITCH

SIT DOWN FOR A SECOND.

?

I WANT TO WORK ON MY OWN GRAPHIC NOVEL. HOW LONG DO I HAVE TO KEEP DOING THESE KINDS OF JOBS?

HOW DO I PUT THIS?

WHAT IF YOU DON'T DO THESE JOBS?

...

THAT GRAPHIC NOVEL YOU WANT SO BAD?

NO ONE'S STOPPING YOU, SO JUST DO IT. IF YOU'RE SO THIRSTY FOR YOUR OWN STORY, I GUESS YOU HAVE TO! WHY NOT?

I HAVE ALL THIS CLEAN AIR AND CAN COLLECT WILD PLANTS AND HUNT FOR FISH. AS LONG AS I HAVE THE DESIRE TO WORK ON A GRAPHIC NOVEL, WHAT'S THE PROBLEM?!

THIS IS NO JOKE... THESE DAYS, I'M WORRIED ABOUT JUST BUYING RICE...

I HAVE A HOUSEHOLD THAT I'M RESPONSIBLE FOR. I CAN'T JUST RUN AWAY FROM LIFE TO WORK ON A GRAPHIC NOVEL.

IF I JUST HAD ENOUGH MONEY TO LIVE A SIMPLE LIFE...

THAT'S NOT RIGHT; DON'T YOU THINK THE COMPOSITION IS A BIT OFF? PLEASE REDO EVERYTHING.

EX-CUSE ME?

IT DOESN'T MATCH THE PREVIOUS PAGES. DON'T YOU THINK YOU'RE BEING TOO CARELESS?

I CARE, AND I WORRY, AND I REALLY DID TRY TO DRAW IT WELL, BUT YOU KEEP DEMANDING TWO, THREE, FOUR MORE CORRECTIONS. I DON'T WANT TO CARE WHEN I DRAW ANYMORE.

I WILL TRY TO DRAW EXACTLY ACCORDING TO YOUR INSTRUCTIONS, SO PLEASE POINT OUT EVERY SINGLE MISTAKE---

I JUST CAN'T.

UGHHHHHHH

AS TEAM LEADER, I EXPECTED YOU TO TAKE BETTER CARE OF THE PROJECT.

I'VE WORKED SO HARD TO ACCOMMODATE YOUR REQUESTS THAT I'VE LOST TOUCH WITH MYSELF.

TEXT: COMIC DRILLS ROBOT

IS IT OKAY TO KEEP LIVING LIKE THIS----

HOW CAN I LIVE IF I NEVER GET TO WORK ON MY OWN BOOK AGAIN?

...HONEY.

IT'S SO QUIET OUT HERE.

ISN'T IT?

TOO QUIET...

HOO-HOOOT

TAK
TAK
TAK

YOU'RE AWAKE ALREADY?

SLURP

MM-HMM.

NOW IT'S CHILLY ALL DAY TOO.

SHIVER

!......

WE'RE ALMOST OUT OF GAS.

THE HOUSE IS BIG, SO WE'LL PROBABLY NEED TWO DRUMS OF PROPANE FOR THE MONTH. THE HEATING COSTS ALONE WILL BE ₩360,000.

IF WE KEEP SHUTTING THE GAS OFF TO SAVE MONEY, THE WINTER'S GOING TO BE HARD.

WAIT!

WHAT IF WE USE COAL? WHEN I WAS A STUDENT, I BURNED COAL BRIQUETTES IN THOSE OLD-FASHIONED FURNACE STOVES.

DOES IT SAVE ON HEATING COSTS?

OF COURSE! YOU CAN'T EVEN COMPARE IT TO PROPANE!

CRACK

WHEW...

LET'S HAVE A LOOK.

...YOU DIDN'T FIX IT?!

I THINK IT LOOKS FINE.

DON'T YOU THINK THIS OTHER PART IS A BIT AWKWARD?

IT IS.

TRY TO FIX IT.

WHY ME?

THE COMPOSITION ISN'T RIGHT, AND WHY IS THE BACKGROUND LIKE THIS HERE?

AND HERE, AND HERE!

I'M ALWAYS TELLING YOU, INDIVIDUALITY IS FINE, BUT FIRST YOU NEED TO STRENGTHEN YOUR DRAWING FUNDAMENTALS SUBSTANTIALLY. THEN YOU CAN SLOWLY DEVELOP YOUR STYLE FOR FUTURE USE...

WHAT, SO YOU TOOK OFF ON YOUR OWN?!

YOU'RE ALWAYS NAGGING ME.

THERE'S OUR HOUSE!

HWEEEEEEEE

MMM...

I'D LIKE TO LIVE HERE FOR A LONG, LONG TIME. HOW ABOUT YOU?

WELL... THEY DID SAY WE COULD STAY AS LONG WE WANTED.

THIS IS JUKYEOP MOUNTAIN.

ON THE EDGE OF THE GWANGNEUNG FOREST—

A CLEAN PLACE, UNTOUCHED BY GRIME—

NO ONE MAY ENTER RECKLESSLY—

THESE TWO CALL IT THEIR CHOSEN FOREST—

국립수목원 입산금지 상수도 보호구역 출입통제

ALL————————

————————OF IT.

SIGNS: NATIONAL ARBORETUM, HIKING PROHIBITED, PROTECTED WATERS, RESTRICTED ACCESS   89

THIS IS OUR GIFT, OPEN ONLY TO THESE TWO PEOPLE ———————

THERE ARE FISH!

IT WOULD BE TASTY IF WE CAUGHT SOME AND TURNED THEM INTO SPICY SOUP.

· · · ·

SMACK

IMAGINE LIVING LIKE THIS EVERY DAY, WITHOUT STRESS OR WORRY.

YEAH...

AND NEXT YEAR, WE CAN HAVE A GARDEN.

WAIT!

WE DON'T HAVE A MOMENT TO WASTE HERE. WE HAVE TO PUT IN AN ORDER FOR COAL BRIQUETTES BEFORE IT GETS COLDER.

TSK...

THE CONTRACT FOR THE NEXT VOLUME IS SETTLED, AND AFTER THEIR COLOR FEE DEDUCTION, WE DON'T HAVE MUCH MONEY LEFT.

246
646
.646
0.646
8.624
0.000
58.000

3001
0900
304

코너에서 현금을 입출금 하실 수

NH nonghyup

WHEW.....

· · ·

THIS IS SO SUFFOCATING. HOW LONG WILL MY ANKLES BE SHACKLED TO THIS WORK?

BEATS ME...

I'M ONLY GETTING OLDER, LIFE KEEPS GOING. I JUMP FROM THIS JOB TO THAT, IN A LIFE HELD CAPTIVE BY LOANS. SO WHEN CAN I WORK ON MY BOOK?

....

IT'S NOT LIKE YOU CAN SIT DOWN AND, SNAP, A GRAPHIC NOVEL APPEARS OVERNIGHT.

IT'S BECAUSE YOU WORK SO SLOWLY. YOU DON'T EVEN REAL-IZE THAT YOU'RE BACKSLIDING INTO OBSCURITY.

THAT'S TRUE.

WHISPER

WHISPER

HONEY, THAT STORE...

HMM? HONEYYY?

SIGN: CHEAP CLOTHING STORE

THERE WASN'T A SINGLE THING I WANTED TO WEAR.

YOU COULD INSTANTLY TELL THAT STORE HAD NOTHING WORTH BUY-ING. WHEN I GET MY NEXT PAYCHECK, I'LL BUY YOU SOME NICE CLOTHES.

STRIDE

WE'LL DELIVER THE STOVE LATER.

...WHERE IN THE AREA DO THEY SELL COAL?

IF YOU DIAL 114, THEY'LL LET YOU KNOW A NEARBY LOCATION.

BARK

BARK!

YOU CAN CHOOSE ONE FROM THE LITTER.

I'LL GO AS LOW AS ₩150,000 FOR A MALE.

EVEN WHEN YOU'RE ALONE, A JINDO DOG WILL BE RELIABLE.

BARK BARK

BARK BARK

WOOF WOOF

I GUESS WE CAN'T JUSTIFY IT RIGHT NOW.

BARK BARK

WOOF

WOOF

THAT PLACE WE LOOKED UP BEFORE IS IN THE AREA. LET'S GO CHECK IT OUT.

BUT JINDOS ARE SUPPOSED TO BE GOOD GUARD DOGS...

HUSH! STOP!

BARK BARK

BARK BARK

YIKES! HOW MANY ABANDONED DOGS ARE THERE?!

WOOF WOOF

BARK

BARK

SIGN: ANIMAL LOVE HUMANE SOCIETY

93

WHAT CAN I DO FOR YOU?

BOW WOW

WE CAME TO LOOK FOR A GUARD DOG.

BARK BARK

WOOF

WELL, THERE ARE DOGS AVAILABLE FOR ADOPTION, AND SOME LOST DOGS AS WELL, SO TAKE YOUR TIME.

OKAY...

BARK

BARK WOOF

HE SAID THE SPAY/NEUTER FEE WAS ₩70,000.

BARK

MM-HMM.

BARK

BARK

BUT SINCE THE REST IS FREE, MIGHT AS WELL TAKE ONE.

WOOF

BARK BARK

THESE ARE ALL THE SMALL DOGS!

THIS WAY...

A DOG THIS SIZE WOULD BE A GREAT GUARD DOG.

HE'S TOO BIG!

PANT PANT

YOU OUGHT TO RAISE A COUPLE OF BIG DOGS TOGETHER.

GOODNESS, TWO OF THEM?

WE ALREADY HAVE THREE CATS, SO THAT'S, UM...

SHOULD WE PICK ONE FROM THIS PEN?

WOOF WOOF

RUFF RUFF

BARK

BARK BARK

WHAT DO YOU THINK OF HIM?

AH, THAT ONE?

HIS COAT IS BLACK, AND HE LOOKS LIKE HE HAS A GOOD DISPOSITION.

HE'S LOOK-ING AT US WITHOUT BARKING.

I RESCUED HIS MOTHER FROM SOME VILLAG-ERS WHO PLANNED TO BUTCHER HER FOR MEAT, BUT THEN SHE TURNED AROUND AND HAD FOUR PUPPIES. HE'S THE LAST OF THE LITTER.

AH...

IT'S PROBABLY BEEN, WHAT, FOUR MONTHS SINCE HE WAS BORN?

REALLY? HE'S ONLY FOUR MONTHS AND HE'S ALREADY THAT BIG?

I'VE NEVER SEEN HIM BARK, NOT ONCE.

95

WELL I LIKE HIM, BUT IF HE DOESN'T BARK, WHAT'S THE POINT?

I KNOW...

WE'LL HAVE TO THINK ABOUT IT AND LET YOU KNOW.

SURE, SURE, COME BACK ANYTIME.

MAN, I WISH SOMEONE WOULD JUST HAND US A JINDO, JUST LIKE THAT...

BANG---

THUD

BANG---

BANG--

BANG

BANG

BANG

HONEY—

SO NOW YOUR LOT IN LIFE IS TO FIELD URGENT PHONE CALLS? WHEN ARE YOU GOING TO DO SOME WORK?

SHUT UP! I'VE GOT TO BUILD A DOGHOUSE IF WE'RE GOING TO BRING ONE HOME!

DELIVERY!

KA-THUNK

DID YOU SAY, "MORE REVISIONS?"

YOU SHOULD ORDER YOUR COAL FAR IN ADVANCE.

WHEN THE SNOW GETS TOO DEEP ON THESE ROADS, THE DELIVERY TRUCK CAN'T MAKE IT UP THE MOUNTAIN.

OH, REALLY?

NICE

CHK

COUGH COUGH

FSHHHHHH

JUST HOW MANY BRIQUETTES HAVE YOU LIT?

SO WEIRD...

S-SO C-C-COLD...

DON'T EXAGGERATE...

OH, COME OVER HERE.

UGH...

. . . .

HUH. WHAT'S THE PROBLEM HERE?

DID THEY MIX IN PHONY BRIQUETTES TO MEET GROWING COAL DEMAND?

SHIT. PLEASE WOULD YOU JUST LIGHT UP!

WE'VE NEARLY GONE THROUGH ALL FORTY BRIQUETTES...

HOOOOO...

WHAT ARE WE GOING TO DO? PROPANE IS TOO EXPENSIVE, AND—

IT'S WARM.

IT'S WARM?!

YEAH... IT IS...

THEY'RE LIT!

YAYYYY!

SHAKE SHAKE

SHAKE

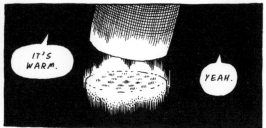

WHOOOOOSH

WHOA...WHOA...
WHOAAAA

STAGGER

CRACK

CRA-ACK

GRUNT!

CRACK

WHEW...

HAAH...

FROM NOW ON, ANYONE WHO COMES UP THIS MOUNTAIN...

WILL KNOW EXACTLY WHO LIVES HERE.

Winter Part 1

THIS ISN'T JAPCHAE; IT'S JUST PURE UNADULTERATED NOODLES.

GRUMBLE GRUMBLE

THERE'S NOTHING WE CAN DO ABOUT IT!

CLATTER CLATTER CLATTER

...THERE ISN'T MUCH RICE LEFT. WE NEED MORE.

MY CONTRACT FEE SHOULD BE DEPOSITED SOON. LET'S HOLD OUT A LITTLE BIT LONGER.

OHHH, REALLY?!

EITHER WAY, WE'RE GOING TO BE SO BUSY FROM NOW ON THAT WE WON'T HAVE TIME TO BLINK OR BREATHE.

I NEED TO START MAKING MONEY TOO...

AGAIN WITH THAT NON-SENSE!

FOCUS ON YOUR ART. THAT'S BETTER THAN WORKING ELSE-WHERE FOR A SMALL AMOUNT OF CASH.

....

THERE'S A FACTORY IN THE AREA; SHOULD WE START PULLING A DOUBLE INCOME?

WHAT?

GIVE ME A BREAK.

HEH HEH HEH

I COULD HELP YOU WITH THE COLORING.

YOU'D BE MORE COMFORTABLE WITH THAT, RIGHT? THEN YOU WOULDN'T HAVE TO PAY THE COLORIST.

FSHHHH...

...I EARN NO MONEY AND MY WIFE WORRIES THAT WE'RE DESTI-TUTE, YET I STILL FIND THE TIME TO GRUMBLE AT HER. I'M AN INCOMPETENT HUSBAND.

PUT YOUR DISHES OVER TO THE SIDE.

CLATTER CLATTER

OKAY.

SURE...

...WE'LL BRING THE BEAST HOME.

HE LOOKS A LITTLE DUMB...YOU THINK HE'LL BE ANY GOOD AT PROTECTING THE HOUSE?

WHAT DO YOU MEAN?

HISSS

- - - - -

HIS BLACK COAT GIVES HIM A STRONG VISUAL PRESENCE.

THIS'LL KEEP HIM WARM, YEAH?

WHAT SHOULD WE NAME HIM?

LET'S CALL HIM OAKIE!

HMM, THAT WAS A LITTLE TOO EASY!

BUT IT'S ONLY NATURAL! THERE ARE SO MANY OAK TREES ON THIS MOUNTAIN—THE TOWN NAME MEANS "OAK-RIDDLED VILLAGE..."

A DOG THAT LIVES HERE IS OAKIE!

HONK HONK

HONEY, OUTSIDE...

WHY ON EARTH ARE THOSE CARS DRIVING UP LIKE THAT?

PICK IT UP!

WHEW! AND HERE I THOUGHT SOMETHING SERIOUS HAD HAPPENED!

WHY DID YOU REACT LIKE THAT?

YOU HAVE TO PUBLICLY SHAME SOMEONE FOR THAT KIND OF BEHAVIOR SO IT DOESN'T HAPPEN AGAIN.

SCRITCH
SCRATCH
SCRATCH

SHIT...

BRRRRIIIING

...

BRRRIIIINNG... BRRRRIINNG... BRIIING

MSM 메신저

담당:
홍작가님
전화좀
받으세요...

DING DING

BRIIING

AREN'T YOU GO-ING TO ANSWER THE PHONE?

DON'T AN-SWER. IT'S MY EDITOR.

BRRRIIIINGG

DING DING

I MEAN, WHAT KIND OF PERSON LETS THE PHONE RING FOR NEARLY A MINUTE?

YANK

HONEY!!

SO YOU'RE GOING TO DO THE BARE MINIMUM AND THEN ACT LIKE THIS, ARE YOU?

YOU GO ON AND ON ABOUT HOW YOU'D RATHER WORK ON YOUR OWN BOOK, BUT WHAT HAVE YOU DONE TO PREPARE FOR THAT EXACTLY?

EVERY DAY YOU SAY YOU'RE GOING TO WRITE, BUT YOU HAVEN'T DONE A THING.

AND NOW YOU'VE GOTTEN TO THE POINT WHERE YOU'RE AVOIDING URGENT PHONE CALLS? WHAT IS THIS?

YOU CAN'T EVEN IMAGINE THE AMOUNT OF HOUSEWORK THAT'S PILED UP SINCE WE'VE MOVED HERE...

ONE DAY IS FILLED WITH SO MANY TASKS: I'VE GOT TO CHANGE OUT THE COAL, FEED THE CATS AND DOG, TAKE OAKIE FOR WALKS, GO OUT FOR GROCERIES. EACH TIME WE GO OUT, THE TRANSPORTATION IS SO INCONVENIENT THAT IT TAKES DOUBLE THE TIME IT DID IN THE CITY.

I DON'T EVEN GET THE CHANCE TO BREATHE BECAUSE I'M SO DAMN BUSY!

BUT THEN, ON THIS SERIES, I GET SADDLED WITH AN EDITOR WHO CHECKS UP ON ME EVERY SINGLE DAY, TO THE POINT OF MADNESS! IS IT ANY WONDER THAT I HAVEN'T MADE ANY PROGRESS ON MY WORK?

THUD

CLACK-CLACK
CLACK
CLACK

ASK TO REDUCE YOUR WORKLOAD. IF WE JUST EAT AND SPEND A LITTLE LESS...

AND WHAT, SUCK ON OUR THUMBS FOR FOOD?

IT'S COLD...IT'S COLD...
IT'S COLD...

SO COLD...SO COLD...
SO COLD...

SO COLD...SO COLD...
SO COLD...

SO CO-!

YOU GUYS!

...AREN'T YOU COLD?

YOU MUST BE COLD, LITTLE GUY.

AND YOUR WATER'S FROZEN.

TA-DAHH!

HURRY AND DRINK SOME. IT'S SO COLD RIGHT NOW.

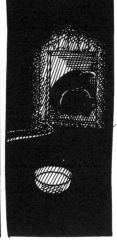

MAN, THE SUBWAY... IT'S BEEN A LONG TIME.

CHA-CHUNG CHA-CHUNG
CHA-CHUNG CHA-CHUNG
CHA-CHUNG

RETCH—

CHA-CHUNG

CHA-CHUNG

THE SMELL OF PEOPLE IS MAKING ME NAUSEOUS...

IT TAKES ALL KINDS, I GUESS.

AIN'T IT COLD UP THERE?

YES, BUT WE HEAT THE HOUSE WITH THE BRIQUETTE STOVE, SO IT'S FINE.

BUT IT MUST BE COLD SO FAR NORTH...

...I'M SORRY WE COULDN'T SEND ANY MONEY THIS MONTH.

NO, NO, IT'S NOTHING LIKE THAT.

OH, WE STILL HAVE MONEY LEFT. DON'T WORRY ABOUT US...ARE Y'ALL ALL RIGHT? NEED US TO SEND SOME MONEY?

BY THE WAY, YOU PROBABLY WON'T BE ABLE TO VISIT MUCH, WILL YA? IT'S SO FAR, AND YOU MUST BE BUSY.

ONCE WE RUN OUT OF KIMCHI, I'LL COME TO VISIT, DAD.

SURE, SURE. I FIGURED YOU WERE NEARLY OUT BY NOW. WELL, COME ON DOWN WHEN YOU RUN OUT.

YO!

I'LL CALL AGAIN SOON.

GOOD-BYE.

IT'S BEEN SO LONG!

RIGHT?!

GLUG

GLUG

GLUG

. . .

WHEN ARE YOU GOING TO INVITE US OUT THERE?

I'LL CALL YOU GUYS WHEN THE HOUSE IS SORTED.

WELL, IT SEEMS LIKE A BEAUTIFUL LOCATION. LOOKING FORWARD TO IT.

AND WORK IS GOING WELL?

I GOT A NEW JOB TO PAY OFF MY SCHOOL FEES.

WHEN WILL YOU RE-ENROLL?

I OUGHT TO NEXT YEAR.

YEAH, YOU HAVE TO GRADUATE WITH US!

BUT YOU LIVE SO FAR NOW, WOULD YOU BE ABLE TO MAKE IT TO CLASS?

ABOUT THAT...

HOUSE

WALK

BUS NO. 11

TOWN BUS NO. 1516

BUS NO. 1222

SCHOOL

IF EVERYTHING RUNS ON TIME, IT'D TAKE...AN HOUR AND A HALF?

IT'S NOT AS BAD AS YOU THINK!

THAT'S ABOUT THE SAME AS ME. IT TAKES AN HOUR AND A HALF TO GET TO SCHOOL FROM HEUKSEOK-DONG.

IT CAN TAKE TWO HOURS WHEN THINGS DON'T RUN ON TIME...

NOW THAT I THINK ABOUT IT, THE THREE OF US HERE...

WE'VE ALL BEEN THROUGH AN APPRENTICESHIP!

YOU'RE RIGHT!

119

APPRENTICESHIPS ARE DYING OUT WITH OUR GENERATION.

SIP

OF COURSE. THE CONCEPT OF ASSISTANTS IS DIFFERENT FROM APPRENTICES.

THESE DAYS, IF YOU DON'T PAY, NO ONE WANTS TO LEARN.

WELL, APPRENTICES EXISTED IN AN ERA OF NAÏVETÉ.

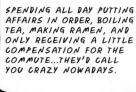

SPENDING ALL DAY PUTTING AFFAIRS IN ORDER, BOILING TEA, MAKING RAMEN, AND ONLY RECEIVING A LITTLE COMPENSATION FOR THE COMMUTE...THEY'D CALL YOU CRAZY NOWADAYS.

PROBABLY!

...I CAN'T BELIEVE WE'RE EVEN TALKING ABOUT THIS.

MAYBE WE'VE GOTTEN OLD.

WHEN DID YOU START DOING COMICS AGAIN?

IT WAS '92, SO...

...IF IT'S 2005 NOW...

IT'S BEEN FOURTEEN YEARS.

...IS THAT RIGHT?

HIC

VISIT US AGAIN SOON—

UGH...I OVERDID IT...

RETCH RETCH

HWOOOOOO . . .

AHEM HM...

♪ I WALKED, THROUGH THE WIND ♫

SONG: "TEA HOUSE IN THE WINTER," (1985) JO YONG-PIL'S HIT TROT BALLAD

EARLY IN THE MORNING, INTO THAT TEA HOUSE—

BARK BARK BARK

WOOF WOOF

WOOF WOOF

BARK BARK BARK

THOSE DAMN MUTTS...

BARK BARK BARK

122

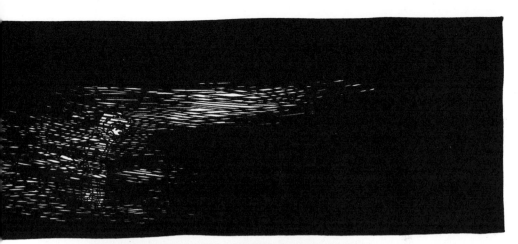

SHHHHHH

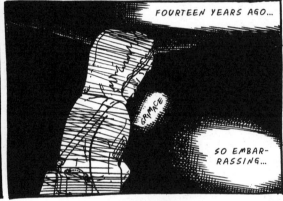

FOURTEEN YEARS AGO...

GRIMACE

SO EMBAR-
RASSING...

IT'S NOT LIKE I'VE
EARNED MUCH MONEY
OR EVEN PRODUCED
A POPULAR SERIES,
AND YET I'M STILL
MAKING A LIVING
OFF COMICS...

THAT ALONE IS A MIRACLE...

124

WHAT ARE YOU DOING? HURRY UP.

CHRIST...

IT'S SO DARK, IT'LL SWALLOW YOU UP.

IS THAT WHY I'M HERE? TO HIDE FROM MY FOURTEEN YEARS OF SHAME?

OR MAYBE I'M HERE TO SHUT MYSELF UP AND COWER IN THE DARK?

...I GUESS IT'S A LITTLE FROM COLUMN A, A LITTLE FROM COLUMN B.

I RELY ON THIS DIM LIGHT...

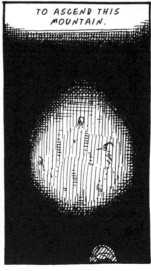

TO ASCEND THIS MOUNTAIN.

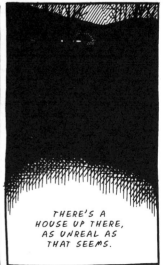

THERE'S A HOUSE UP THERE, AS UNREAL AS THAT SEEMS.

IN THAT ISOLATED HOUSE, A WOMAN WHO I CALL MY WIFE...

WAITS FOR HER HUSBAND...

LIKE A DISTANT DREAM.

I'M SORRY, I LET THE BRIQUETTES BURN OUT...

OH!

DID YOU AND YOUR FRIENDS HAVE A GOOD TIME?

MM-HMM.

CAN YOU TAKE A LOOK AT THE WORK I DID TONIGHT?

I'M TIRED. LET'S LOOK AT IT TOMORROW.

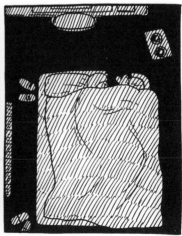

THEY SAY THAT FULL-BLOWN WINTER BEGINS TOMORROW. WE'LL SEE THE MORNING TEMPERATURES PLUMMET TO FREEZING.

IT'S ALREADY THE END OF THE YEAR, AND I'M SURE YOU'LL ALL BE VERY BUSY WITH YEAR-END CELEBRATIONS.

BUT IT'S GREAT TO HAVE FRIENDS TO GATHER WITH BEFORE THE YEAR PASSES.

AND THE MOST FITTING SONG REQUEST FOR THE LAST DAY OF NOVEMBER IS...

LET'S EAT!

MMM.

YOU MUST BE GETTING INTO THE SWING OF THINGS.

NOW THAT THE DEADLINE IS RIGHT IN FRONT OF MY NOSE, I CAN ACTUALLY CONCENTRATE.

I'VE BEEN THINKING OF SHAVING MY HEAD...

BUT IT'S SUPPOSED TO BE MUCH COLDER STARTING TOMORROW!

I DON'T FEEL LIKE GOING ALL THE WAY TO THE CITY JUST TO GET MY HAIR CUT...

YOU LIKE BEING OUTSIDE IN THESE WIDE OPEN SPACES AFTER BEING COOPED UP IN THE DOGHOUSE, HUH?

PANT PANT

LOOK AT HIM, HE COULDN'T EVEN WALK THAT WELL IN THE BEGINNING, BUT NOW HE'S SO RAMBUNCTIOUS.

RUFF RUFF RUFF

LOOK AT YOU! YOU'RE BARKING NOW!

RUFF

RUFF

RUFF

THAT MEANS YOU LIKE IT HERE, HUH?

ALL RIGHT. THAT SETTLES IT. I'M GOING TO WRITE A CHARMING STORY BASED ON YOU!

PANT PANT PANT

WE CAME HERE BECAUSE WE HATED THE SUFFOCATING CITY, AND YOU CAME HERE AFTER YOU FLED THOSE PRISON BARS!

PANT PANT PANT

?

I MEAN, IF YOU LIKE IT SO MUCH HERE, IT MUST BE THE SAME FOR US, RIGHT?

OF COURSE!

TAP

TIME TO WRAP UP THIS BASTARD OF A JOB AND DIVE INTO MY OWN WORK!

TAKE YOUR TIME COMING UP WITH THE CONCEPT...

AND WHILE THE SUN'S STILL OUT.

HMM?

BZZZ

ZZZZZZ

131

...NOW THAT IT'S ALL SAID AND DONE, YOU MISS IT, DON'T YOU?

I FEEL REFRESHED!

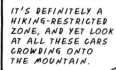
IT'S DEFINITELY A HIKING-RESTRICTED ZONE, AND YET LOOK AT ALL THESE CARS CROWDING ONTO THE MOUNTAIN.

GRIP

GRIP

GRIP

FLICK

FLICK

FLICK

—THE HELL!

IT'S FINE IF THEY WANT TO ENJOY A BIT OF HIKING NOW AND THEN...

BUT IF I LET THAT GO ON, THEY'LL KEEP LITTERING AND PISSING ME OFF...

HEY NOW! ENOUGH OF THAT! GET BACK TO WORK.

IT'S MORE IMPORTANT. DON'T WASTE YOUR TIME GOING OUTSIDE.

YEAH, YOU STAY RIGHT THERE.

I'LL GO IN YOUR PLACE.

YOU LISTEN TO YOUR WIFE!

WE NEED TO BLOCK THE ROAD OR SOMETHING.

ISN'T THAT A GOOD IDEA?

SHAKE SHAKE

HANG ON A SECOND.

YOU'RE PROBABLY HUNGRY, SO WHY DON'T YOU HAVE A BITE TO EAT?

MAYBE I WILL.

THINK IT'LL SNOW SOON?

SMACK SMACK

PROBABLY.

WHEN DO YOU HAVE TO TURN IN YOUR WORK?

LATE MARCH.

NOM NOM

YOU STILL HAVE SOME LEEWAY.

IF IT'S SELECTED IN THE COMPETITION, THEY'LL EVEN SEND ME TO DENMARK, LAND OF HANS CHRISTIAN ANDERSEN.

WOW!

THAT'D BE AWESOME!

YOU CAN SURVIVE WITHOUT ME FOR A WEEK, RIGHT?

HUH?

YOU'D BE GONE THAT LONG?

I'D WANT TO STOP BY FRANCE TOO.

WE'RE GETTING AHEAD OF OUR-SELVES! THE DEADLINE'S STILL FAR OFF.

PA HA HA

HAHAHA

....

....

CLATTER

CLACK

YOU
LITTLE—

HEY!

PANT
PANT
PANT

SLOW DOWN!

DON'T
BE SO
ILL-MAN-
NERED!

BONK

LOOK AT HOW STRAIGHT
HIS TAIL IS. HE'S IN THE
BEST MOOD WHEN HE'S
ON A WALK. DON'T BE
SO HARD ON HIM.

PANT

PANT

LET'S BUY
A CAR!

LIVING WITHOUT A CAR OUT IN THE COUNTRY IS TOO MUCH TROUBLE. IF WE GET ANY EXTRA CASH, LET'S BUY A CAR.

A USED ONE THAT COSTS ₩1,000,000!

WHY DO YOU NEED A CAR WHEN THERE'S THE BUS? AND WHERE DO WE GET THAT KIND OF MONEY?

IT'S ALREADY HARD ENOUGH WALKING DOWN THE MOUNTAIN...

DOES THE BUS EVER EVEN SHOW UP AT THE RIGHT TIME?

REDUCING THE TRAVEL TIME TO SEOUL BY HALF AN HOUR IS EARNING MONEY TOO.

WELL, WE CAN'T. LET'S THINK ABOUT IT AFTER WE PAY OFF OUR DEBT.

OUR LATE HEALTH INSURANCE PAYMENTS HAVE ADDED UP.

THAT'S A SEPARATE MATTER. IN REALITY, YOU KNOW WE DESPERATELY NEED A CAR NOW!

HMM...

THEN AT LEAST A MOTORCYCLE! WHEN WE GO OUT FOR GROCERIES, WE CAN EXPEDITE OUR TRIPS TO THE BUS STATION!

THERE HE GOES...

RAGE

WELL I'M DECIDED!!

WE HAVE TO!

WHINE!

GET OVER HERE!

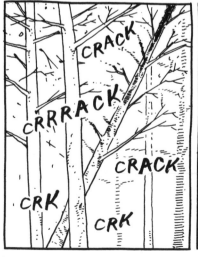

TAP TAP TAP

TAP   TAP

- - -

- - -

IT'S
SNOWING!

NOW THAT IT'S SNOWING,
SHOULD I WHIP UP
SOMETHING TASTY?

WHEW,
IT'S
COLD!

ARE YOU
DONE?

LET'S SEE...

WHAT DO WE
GOT? NOW
THAT IT'S
SNOWING...

SQUEAK

142

IT'S BEEN SO LONG SINCE WE'VE BEEN TO THE MARKET...THERE AREN'T ANY INGREDIENTS.

SHUT

LET'S JUST EAT RICE FOR DINNER.

WHAT?

YOU SPENT TOO MUCH TIME PILING UP STONES AND LOGS TO BUILD THE RETAINING WALL. WEREN'T YOU GOING TO GET THROUGH A BUNCH OF DRAWINGS TODAY?

WELLLLL, AS LONG AS I FINISH AND UPLOAD THEM BY TONIGHT...

HAVE IT YOUR WAY.

OH...

THE ONE THING WE DO HAVE IS FLOUR...

KNEAD

KNEAD

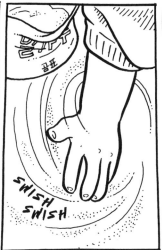

SWISH

SWISH

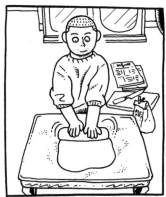

145

146

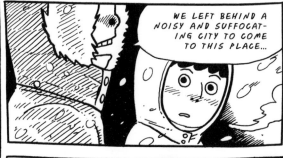

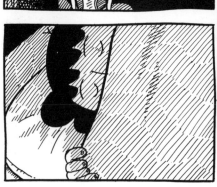

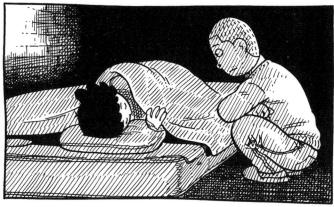

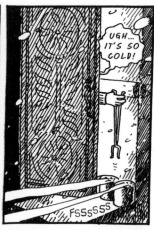

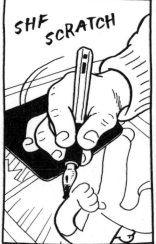

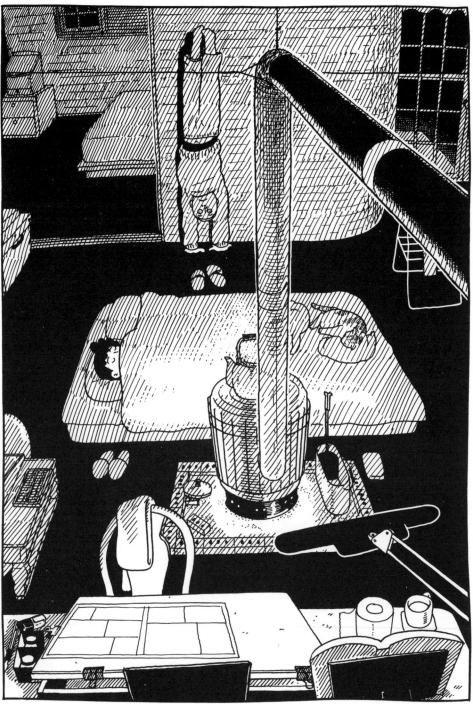

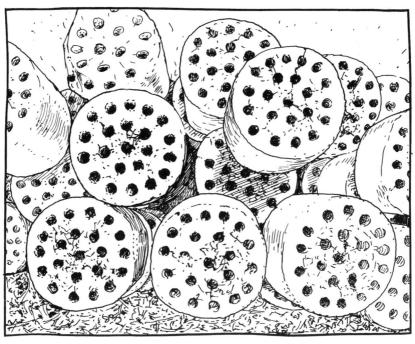

Winter Part 2

CLACK

HELLO?

YES...OKAY...

HE ISN'T UP YET.

WHEN HE WAKES UP, I'LL TELL HIM TO CALL YOU.

....

YES, WHEN HE WAKES UP, I'LL LET HIM KNOW YOU CALLED. YES, GOODBYE.

EDITOR?

CLICK

THERE'S SOMETHING OFF ABOUT HER. WHEN I TOLD HER YOU'D CALL BACK, SHE KEPT INSISTING I WAKE YOU UP.

WOBBLE

BUT I FINISHED THE MANU-SCRIPT AND UPLOADED IT BEFORE I WENT TO BED...

YAWWWN

CHEW CHEW

...

ARE YOU SURE THIS IS KIMCHI STEW?

SMACK SMACK

...YOU FORGOT THE DRIED ANCHOVY, DIDN'T YOU?

IS IT SO IMPORTANT?

HOW CAN YOU LEAVE OUT THE ANCHOVIES AND USE ONLY KIMCHI AND CALL IT A STEW?

YOU'VE SEEN ME BOIL ANCHOVIES TO MAKE THE STEW BASE.

ALL RIGHT. I'LL USE THEM NEXT TIME.

CHOMP CHOMP

CHOMP

CHOMP CHOMP CHOMP

GRUMBLE GRUMBLE

PURRRRR...

BRRIIINNG...

BRRRIINNNG...

.....

HELLO?

YES, IT'S ME. I HAVE SOME REVISIONS TO GO OVER.

I'M EATING BREAK-FAST RIGHT NOW. I'LL CALL YOU WHEN I'M DONE.

IT'LL ONLY TAKE A MINUTE. I'LL JUST TELL YOU THE SECTIONS THAT NEED REVISING.

I SAID, I'M IN THE MID-DLE OF EATING.

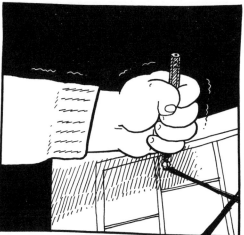

WHAT THE HELL...

SHE MIGHT AS WELL HAVE TOLD ME
TO REDRAW THE ENTIRE THING.

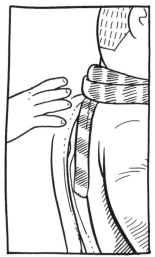

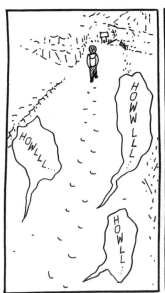

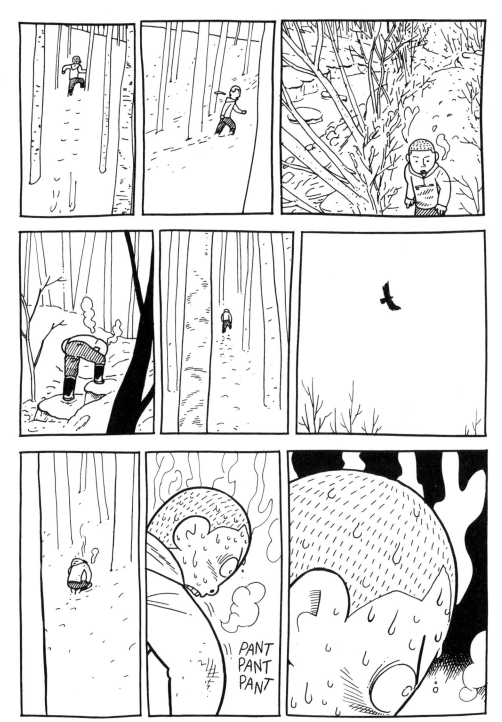

YOU'RE BULLSHIT-
TING ME RIGHT NOW,
AREN'T YOU? WHEN
ARE YOU GOING TO
FINISH?

SHOULDN'T THE AU-
THOR BE CONCERNED
WITH THE QUALITY OF
THE WORK AND NOT
JUST THE ROYALTIES?

ERGH!

POW POW POW

POW POW

THUMP

ARGH!

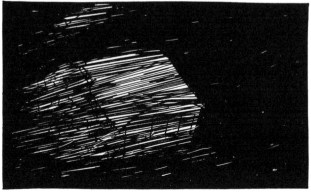

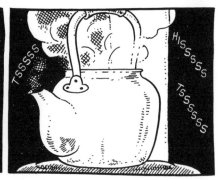

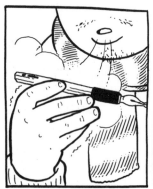

IT'S ACTUALLY WARMER, NOW THAT WE'VE BLOCKED HALF THE SPACE. WE SHOULD HAVE THOUGHT OF THAT SOONER, EH?

YEAH.

THE PROBLEM IS THE LIVING ROOM. THIS WEAK COAL STOVE CAN'T BURN OFF THE MOISTURE LIKE THE GAS BOILER USED TO, SO MILDEW IS STARTING TO APPEAR...

I'M AWARE.

WE DON'T HAVE MUCH FUEL LEFT EITHER.

WE'VE RUN OUT OF KIMCHI TOO, SO I'LL HEAD TO SEOUL TO GET SOME MORE.

I'LL ALSO STOP BY KYUNGDONG MARKET TO GRAB SOME STAPLES.

WHAT ABOUT MONEY?

I'VE GOT ABOUT ₩20,000, SO I SHOULD BE ABLE TO PAY FOR SOME FOOD...FOR THE TIME BEING.

AHHH—I WISH I COULD EARN SOME MONEY TOO—

YOU SHOULD BE MORE CONCERNED WITH MAKING THE COMPETITION DEADLINE.

MORE NAGGING!

THBTHB

BRRRIING-
BRRRIIING-

HELLO?

HANG ON A SECOND.

HONEY.

WHO?

MR. CHANG CHANG.

HEY, WHEN ARE YOU COMING BACK TO SEOUL?

CAN'T JIHOON JOIN US?

SIZZLE   SIZZLE

DON'T YOU KNOW HOW FAR POCHEON IS FROM HERE?

YEAH? IT MUST BE SO QUIET UP THERE. FRESHER AIR TOO...

YOU MUST LIKE IT.

I'D LIKE TO VISIT, BUT I DON'T KNOW WHEN THIS JOB WILL END...

OH YEAH, IS GOLDIE DOING OKAY?

CLINK

...OH YEAH, GOLDIE'S DOING GREAT.

SURE, SURE, YOU GUYS HAVE A GOOD TIME, ALL RIGHT?

SOUNDS FUN.

ALL MY ART SCHOOL FRIENDS MUST HAVE GOTTEN TOGETHER.

tsk

....

YOU SHOULD JOIN THEM!

DON'T WORRY ABOUT IT. I HAVE TOO MUCH TO DO.

MAYBE I'LL DO A LITTLE EXERCISE?

WITH YOUR COLD? ARE YOU KIDDING ME?!

LET'S GO OUT TOGETHER.

?

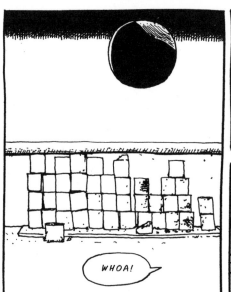

IT'S ADDRESSED TO THE NEIGHBORS, BUT WE COULD HOLD ON TO IT FOR THEM, YEAH?

OH MAN, ALL THIS MOVING AROUND IS MAKING ME HUNGRY.

YOU TOO?

MEAT! I WANNA EAT MEAT!

FLIP

VOILA

MONEY?!

GRIN

SAVINGS!

SAVE IT FOR CAB FARE, HONEY.

GRRRUMBLE

LET'S GO.

MY FARE CARD STILL HAS A BALANCE, SO LET'S EAT.

STEP
STEP STEP

IT'LL BE DELICIOUS IF WE ROAST IT OVER THE FIRE.

THE SHOULDER MEAT IS ABOUT ₩10,000, PLUS THE WIRE GRILL... WITH TWO BOTTLES OF RICE WINE...WE SPENT MOST OF THE ₩20,000?! WE'D BETTER WALK...

AT LEAST WE GOT EVERY-THING WE NEEDED.

OH!

LOOK AT THAT BIRD. HE LOOKS LIKE HE'S CALMLY SWIMMING THROUGH THE SKY WITH HIS WINGS SPREAD LIKE THAT!

IT'S A BIRD OF PREY. PROBABLY A HAWK.

WOW—IT'S SO COOL!

WILD GOSLINGS CAN JUST LOOK AT THE SHADOW OF A BIRD FLYING ABOVE AND KNOW WHETHER IT'S A PREDATOR. ISN'T THAT SOMETHING?

HOW DO THEY KNOW?

A SHORT NECK AND LONG TAIL SIGNIFIES A PREDATOR, AND A LONG NECK WITH A SHORT TAIL IS NOTHING TO WORRY ABOUT.

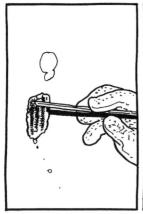

SHAKE
SHAKE

WHAT
SHOULD
WE TOAST
TO?

TO YOU AND ME
LIVING LONG, LONG,
HEALTHY LIVES!

CHEERS!

CLINK

KYAAAHHH,
THAT TASTES
GREAT!!

LICK
LICK

HOO-HOOOOT

HOOOT

HOO-HOOOOT

MAN—I'M DRUNK—

AND COLD.

THERE'S NO ONE BUT US...

THERE'S NO ONE BUT US ON THIS MOUNTAIN...

IT WOULDN'T BE A STRETCH TO SAY THAT BEING TRAPPED BEHIND THIS MOUNTAIN FEELS OTHERWORLDLY...

BURRP

OUR TIME IS FREE HERE, AND WE CAN FORGET HOW GRIMY THE REST OF THE WORLD IS.

AND SOMEHOW, BECAUSE OF THAT, I'VE BEEN WORKING SO WELL...

HONEY, I THINK YOU'VE BEEN FEELING THIS WAY BECAUSE WORK HAS BEEN EXHAUSTING.

BUT MOVING HERE WAS THE RIGHT THING TO DO.

WOOF!

PANT PPNTPANT

TASTY, HUH? IT'S FIRE-GRILLED!

SMACK
SNARF
CHOMP CHOMP

...YOUR WATER'S FROZEN AGAIN?

CLANG
CLANG

THUNK

....

WHAT ARE YOU WAITING FOR? DRINK UP WHILE IT'S WARM.

IT'S NOT TOO HOT.

SNIFF SNIFF

DON'T WANT ANY?

WHINE

DRINK WHEN YOU FEEL LIKE IT, THEN.

MAN, IT'S COLD!

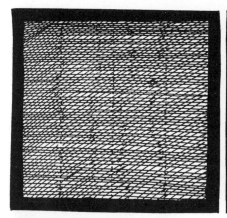

♪ AT THE SEASHORE

WHERE THE RUGOSA
ROSE DELICATELY
BLOOMS...

IF I WALK ALONE
THE HORIZON IS
FAR AWAY— ♫

SONG: "AT THE SEASHORE," IS A CHILDREN'S NURSERY RHYME

♪ TWO PAIRS OF SEAGULLS
APPEAR HAZY,
THE WAVES ARE GENTLE—

AT THE SEASHORE

SCAN

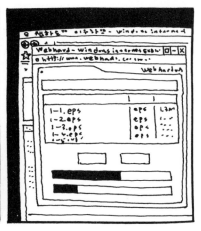

WHEW—IT'S OVER.

CLATTER CLATTER

THE KIMCHI WE'RE HAVING WITH BREAKFAST IS THE LAST OF IT.

OKAY.

HONEY...

HMM?

LEAN

AFTER WE PAY OFF ALL THE BILLS AND EXPENSES WITH THE BOOK MONEY, WE'RE LEFT WITH ABOUT ₩700,000.

WE CAN'T GET A CAR!

PSH, WHAT KIND OF CAR COULD YOU EVEN GET WITH SO LITTLE CASH?

WE CAN'T GET A MO- TORBIKE EITHER!

HA HA HA...

VROOM VROOOM

VRRRO OOOOOM

RIDE, BABY, RIDE!

BUT IN THE END, SHE GAVE IN.

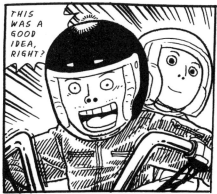

THIS WAS A GOOD IDEA, RIGHT?

I CAN'T HEAR YOU!

I SAID, THIS WAS A GOOD IDEA!

NOW THIS CHARIOT WILL TAKE US ANYWHERE, ANYTIME.

IT'S SO NICE THAT WE CAN COME TO CAFES LIKE THIS NOW, THANKS TO THAT BIKE.

THERE ARE LOTS OF PLACES TO VISIT IN POCHEON, SO LET'S EXPLORE EVERYTHING.

PROMISE!

AW, DO WE REALLY NEED TO PINKY-SWEAR?

SIGN: GOMORI CAFE VILLAGE

PROMISE ME YOU'LL NEVER SELL THE MOTORCYCLE, NO MATTER HOW LITTLE MONEY WE'VE GOT.

BECAUSE YOU LIKE IT SO MUCH.

OKAY!

BRRIING

YES?

IT LOOKS LIKE YOU HAVEN'T UPLOADED THE MANUSCRIPT YET!

I'M ABOUT TO FINISH A DIFFERENT MANUSCRIPT SO I HAVEN'T BEEN ABLE TO WORK ON YOURS YET.

WOULD YOU PLEASE GIVE US SOME MORE CONSIDERATION?

THE MANUSCRIPTS YOU'VE BEEN SUBMITTING LATELY LACK SINCERITY. THERE'S NO SOUL IF YOU JUST COPY THE AUTHOR'S THUMBNAILS SO PRECISELY.

EVEN IF I TRY TO PRODUCE IT MY WAY, I STILL END UP HAVING TO REDRAW THE ENTIRE PAGE THREE, FOUR TIMES.

AND IF WE'RE GOING TO GO DOWN THAT ROAD, DO I REALLY NEED TO SPEND SO MUCH TIME PUNCHING UP THOSE TEMPLATES?

UGH, I'LL DO WHATEVER YOU WANT. JUST POINT OUT WHAT YOU WANT REVISED.

THAT'S NOT WHAT I WANT!

....

HONEY, WHY ARE YOU STANDING THERE, HOLDING THE PHONE LIKE THAT?

IT'S ANOTHER SILENT PROTEST.

HANG ON A SEC.

YOU GUYS COME OUT HERE A MOMENT.

SHK

YANK

WHAT THE HELL?

VROOOOM...

DID YOU FORGET ANYTHING?

I'VE GOT THE BRAISED PEPPERS, KIMCHI, SEAWEED, PICKLES... THAT'S EVERYTHING.

YOU PACKED TOFU TOO? BUT WE CAN BUY THAT ANYTIME.

Y'ALL NEED A CAR SO YOU CAN GO BACK AND FORTH COMFORTABLY.

...WE DO NEED ONE.

I SHOULD STILL BE WORKIN' AND EARNIN' ME AN INCOME, BUT I CAN'T EVEN HELP OUT, AND WELL, YOU KNOW...

C'MON, DAD...

BEEP BEEP

TURN UP YOUR BOILER. YOUR FLOOR IS BARELY LUKEWARM.

DON'T YOU WORRY 'BOUT US. ALL WE NEED IS A BLANKET ON THE FLOOR.

CITY BOILERS DON'T WORK TOO GOOD ANYWAY.

SIGN: CHEONGNYANGNI WHOLESALE PRODUCE MARKET

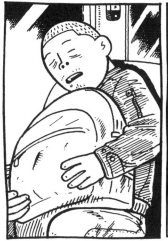

PA-
HS-
HS-
HS-
SHK

?

SK-
SK-
SKREEE-

BWOOOAA AAM

PUH-SH-SH-
SH...

WHAT'S WRONG WITH THIS THING?

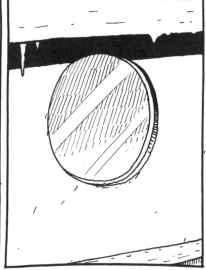

SHIVER

DAMN...IT FEELS LIKE ALL THE MOISTURE IS LEAKING OUT OF MY BODY.

AT THIS RATE, I'M GOING TO TURN INTO JERKY!

HONEY, EAT SOMETHING, AND LET'S GET YOU TO THE DOCTOR. C'MON!

. . . . .

GRUMBLE

GRUMBLE

EVEN IF YOU HAVE NO APPETITE, YOU NEED TO EAT TO GET BETTER.

I'M BEHIND ON WORK, BUT MY BODY WON'T COOPERATE WITH ME.

I'LL DO THE DISHES...

CLATTER CLATTER

YOU JUST GET READY TO GO TO THE DOCTOR!

WHAT ARE YOU DOING? WE NEED TO GO NOW.

. . . . .

I JUST DON'T KNOW.

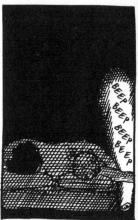

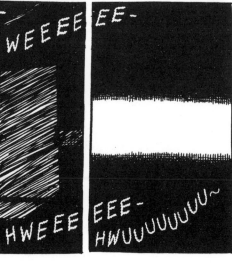

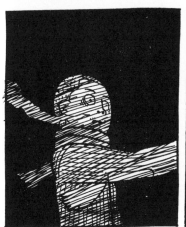

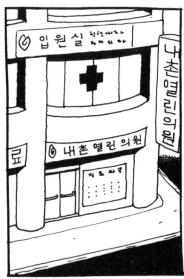

YOU NEED FULL REST. I'LL GIVE YOU A SHOT NOW, AND PRESCRIBE YOU TWO DAYS OF MEDICATION.

STARE

WHEN YOU'RE SICK, A SHOT WILL CURE WHAT AILS YA!

DON'T ACT SO INNO-CENT!

NOW LET'S EARN SOME GODDAMN MONEY!!

SHF SHF SHF SHF SHF SHF SHF SHF

CASH!

CASH!

CASH!

CASH!

NOW HOLD ON! YOU'RE GOING OVERBOARD AGAIN. YOU ALREADY TOOK YOUR MEDICINE, SO GET SOME REST TODAY, AND WORK AGAIN TOMORROW.

MEOW

IT'S FINE. IN THIS CONDITION, TAKING A BREAK WOULD BE AN UTTER WASTE.

HEY, FRIENDS!

197

WHATEVER THE EDITORIAL DEPARTMENT WANTS, WE WILL EXECUTE, GOT IT?!

DON'T WORRY—YOU MAY HAVE DRAWN US, BUT WE'LL END UP OBEYING ANY AND ALL COMMANDS FROM EDITORIAL ANYWAY.

MEANWHILE, WE'D LIKE IT IF YOU'D RENDER US EXACTLY AS ORDERED!

OH, THERE AREN'T VERY MANY REVISIONS THIS TIME.

GOOD WORK.

...HOW ARE BOOK SALES GOING?

THEY'RE BEING RELEASED INTO CIRCULATION CONTINUALLY, BUT WE'LL HAVE TO WAIT AND SEE.

I HOPE YOU CAN HANG IN THERE WITH JUST THE BASE ROYALTIES FOR NOW...

SIGH...THIS IS BECOMING TOO FREQUENT, BUT WE ARE PAYING YOU THE MANUSCRIPT FEE MINUS THE FREE-LANCE COLORING FEES...

POP

BUT YOU SHOULD HAVE MATCHED THE COLORIST'S PAY SCALE TO THE REST OF THE BUDGET.

WHAT BUDGET?! FOR FOUR OR FIVE MONTHS OF BOOK FEES, MINUS THE INKING AND COLORING FEES, I'LL BE LUCKY IF I'M LEFT WITH EVEN ₩200,000!!!

NYEH

WELL, JOBS THAT PAY IN ROYALTIES ARE A ZERO-SUM GAME. YOU REALLY OUGHT TO HAVE STARTED THIS WORK WITH SOME SAVINGS UNDER YOUR BELT.

OH, PLEASE. LET'S JUST TRY TO SETTLE THE NEXT VOLUME'S CONTRACT EARLIER SO I CAN GET PAID AND PAY OFF THE REST OF THIS VOLUME'S COLORING FEES.

IT'S KIND OF COLD...

SHIVER

YOU'RE PUSHING TOO HARD. IF YOU WANT TO FULLY RECOVER, YOU HAVE TO REST.

HOW'S YOUR WORK GOING?

POUR

EH, IT'S SO-SO. NOW GO TO SLEEP.

AH, THE COALS!

I COULD REPLACE THE BRIQUETTES...

IT'S MY JOB.

I WISH WINTER WOULD JUST END ALREADY...

199

200

SHHH...

WHY YOU LITTLE!!

PTOO
PTEH
PTEH

PANT

PANT

FSHHH...

ZZZZZ...

I'M GOING TO NEED THREE OR FOUR MORE POTFULS.

COUGH

HONEY, WAKE UP, WILLYA?!

ZZZ...

DO YOU KNOW WHAT TIME IT IS ALREADY?

IT'S TIMES LIKE THESE THAT IT WOULD BE NICE IF SOMEONE MADE ME SOME BREAKFAST...

203

THE SNOW IS REALLY COMING DOWN! LET'S GO OUTSIDE AND PLAY!!

YEAH?!

I'M BUSY.

FINE, I'LL GO BY MYSELF.

DO WHATEVER YOU WANT.

SCRATCH SCRATCH

BAM

SCRITCH SCRATCH SCRITCH

I HAVE TO FINISH THIS BEFORE THE WEEKEND.

SCRATCH SCRATCH

CHRIST...HAVE I BEEN WORKING TOO HARD ALL DAY?

THROB THROB

. . .

. . .

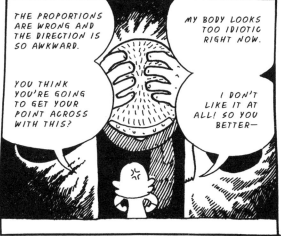

206

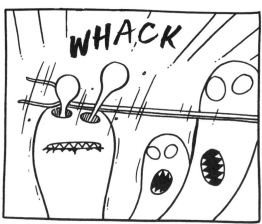

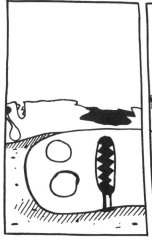

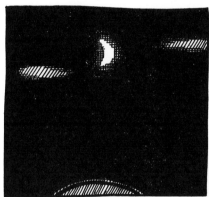

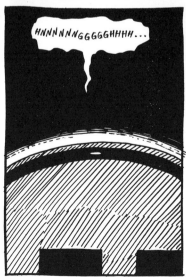

THA-
THUNK
THUNK

CRACK
CRACK
CRACK

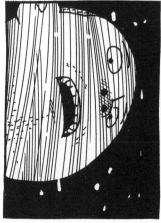

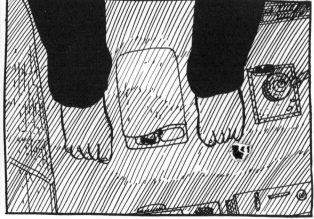

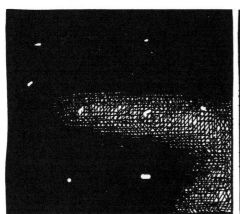

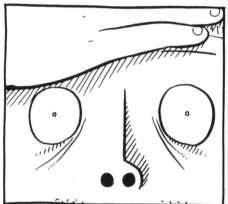

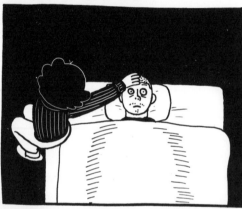

HWEEEEEEEEE

WE ARE BURIED, WINTERS-
DEEP INSIDE THE MOUNTAIN.

Winter Part 3

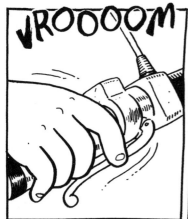

WE MISSED THE LAST BUS BACK TO NAECHON...

TAXI...

MAYBE WE CAN GRAB A CAB...

PASSENGERS HEADED TO NAECHON, PLEASE BOARD!

내촌 참숯 가마
031 - 7000 - 1111

FOR REAL?!

...LET'S ASK, AND IF IT'S CHEAPER THAN A TAXI, LET'S TAKE IT.

THIS IS JUST A FREE SERVICE THAT OFFERS RIDES TO LOCAL RESIDENTS. HOP IN!

WOW!

WAIT A SECOND.

?

수
퍼

SIGN: SUPERMARKET

HONEY!

BRUSH
BRUSH

BITA
500

PLEASE ACCEPT THIS ENERGY DRINK AS THANKS FOR DRIVING US.

YOU'RE NOT HURT?

LOOK AT THE BLOOD ON YOUR HANDS!

I CAN JUST CLEAN IT OFF.

I WAS TRYING TO EX-PRESS MY GRATITUDE, BUT I THINK I JUST MADE HIM UNCOM-FORTABLE.

NO WAY.

THE PEOPLE WHO MISS THE LAST BUS AFTER MIDNIGHT IN NAECHON HAVE A HARD TIME FINDING A TAXI.

IT'S WARM.

BRRINNG
BRRRRIIIING
BRRIIING

YOU HAVE TO BE PREPARED TO WAIT. SOMETIMES THE CABS RECEIVE CALLS BEFORE THEY EVEN REACH THE TAXI STAND, AND THEY HAVE TO GO BACK IN THE DIRECTION THEY CAME FROM.

IT'S HERE!

SCREECH

TAXI

OH, BY THE WAY, WHERE ARE YOU HEADED?

OH UH, MAW-MEE-YUNG-LEE? MAW-MEEYUNGLEE!

MAMYEONGRI IS IN THE SAME DIRECTION AS US!

LET'S SHARE THIS CAB!

THANKS TO YOU SO VERY MUCH.

TAXI

THE MOTORCYCLE WAS MODEST, AND SO WAS THE MONEY WE MADE SELLING IT.

WE CAN PAY OUR RENT AND OVERDUE BILLS; I TRY AND CALCULATE WHAT MONEY MIGHT BE LEFT OVER.

SMOOTH

OUR CELL PHONE SERVICE HAS BEEN CANCELLED, AND NOW THEY'RE SAYING THEY'RE GOING TO DISCONNECT OUR LAND LINE.

WE HAVE TO DO SOMETHING! ARE YOU JUST GOING TO KEEP SITTING HERE LIKE THAT?

HONEY!

YOU CAN'T TALK TO A PERSON WHO'S LOST HIS MIND!

HE'S IN A STATE OF TOTAL ANGER.

BEING STRAPPED FOR CASH IS DEFINITELY WORTH STRESSING OVER, ESPECIALLY SINCE IT'S NOT JUST HIM ANYMORE.

BUT THE REST DOESN'T WARRANT SUCH CONCERN.

HE SHOULD FINISH THE WORK HE'S CONTRACTUALLY OBLIGED TO DO, PROMPTLY. THAT'S HIS PROMISE AND RESPONSIBILITY.

HM...HM...HM...

HM...HM...HM...

WOBBLE

WOBBLE

HM...HM...HM... HM...HM...

HE'S NOT IN A GOOD STATE.

WOBBLE WOBBLE

YEAH, LET'S LEAVE HIM ALONE.

I'M HUNGRY...

I'LL MAKE YOU DINNER. JUST WAIT A BIT.

NO!

I WANT TO EAT HOTTEOK,* THE KIND YOU EAT AT THE FAIR...

*PANCAKE FILLED WITH BROWN SUGAR OR HONEY 223

HONEY...WHAT'S... WHAT'S WRONG WITH ME?

I'VE BEEN SEIZED BY SOME UNKNOWN ANGER FROM WHO KNOWS WHERE...

I JUST LIKED TO DRAW...JUST... THAT'S ALL...

NOW I FIND MYSELF HATING COMICS.

I THINK...IT'S PUSHING ME AWAY... WHAT DO I DO?

AND THIS LIFE WE'RE LIVING IS TOO EXHAUSTING...

I SHOVE MY NOSTRILS ABOVE THE SURFACE OF THE WATER TO BREATHE, BUT I ALWAYS SINK TO THE BOTTOM...LIVING LIKE THIS, ON THE RAZOR'S EDGE...

WHENEVER I THINK, "I CAN'T DO THIS," I OPEN UP THE MAN- USCRIPT TO WORK, BUT THEN I'M PLAGUED BY ALL THOSE INSANE REVISIONS.

225

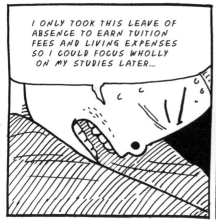

I ONLY TOOK THIS LEAVE OF ABSENCE TO EARN TUITION FEES AND LIVING EXPENSES SO I COULD FOCUS WHOLLY ON MY STUDIES LATER...

ENOUGH!

NO MORE!

YOU CAN'T KEEP GOING ON WITH THIS NEGATIVE TRAIN OF THOUGHT.

EVEN THOUGH IT MIGHT BE DIFFICULT... THE THING YOU NEED TO DO RIGHT NOW IS FINISH YOUR WORK.

BEFORE THE PHONE RINGS!

AS FOR ANY MONEY WE NEED RIGHT NOW, I'LL DO WHAT I CAN TO GET SOME.

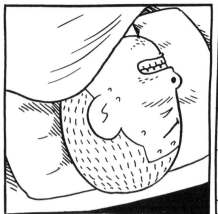

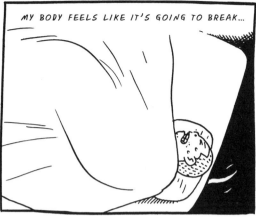

MY BODY FEELS LIKE IT'S GOING TO BREAK...

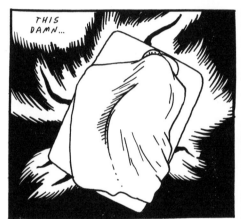

THIS
DAMN...

THIS DAMN MOUNTAIN...

I NEED TO GET OFF
THIS MOUNTAIN...

SIGN: ADMINISTRATION

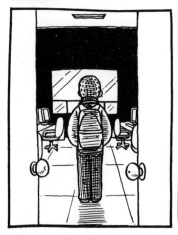

228

...FRUIT!

BOOM———

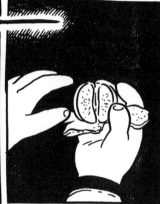

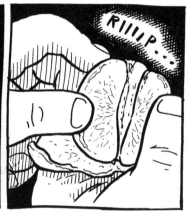

RIIIIP...

BOOM——

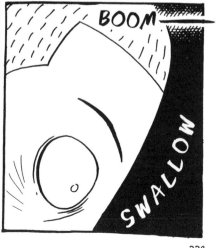

BOOM——

SWALLOW

HELLO.

IT'S ME.

WHY DO YOU SOUND LIKE THAT? DID SOMETHING HAPPEN?

HAVE A TASTE. IT'S CHEAP.

YEAH...UM...

THIS HERE WAS DRIED BY HAND.

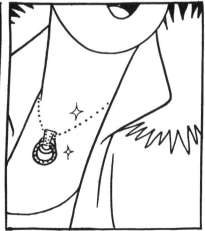

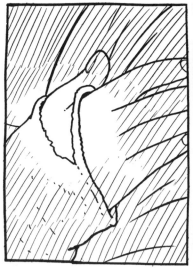

SAID THE FOX TO THE LITTLE PRINCE.

DING...

I THOUGHT YOU WERE BUSY; WHAT BRINGS YOU ALL THE WAY HERE?

OH...I, UH...

THESE...

I'LL SEE YOU AFTER WORK!

SAID THE FOX TO THE LITTLE PRINCE.

WARM, RIGHT?

YES.

I DON'T HAVE ANYTHING FOR YOU THOUGH...

I'LL WALK YOU BACK TO THE OFFICE.

WHEW

IT'S DARK ENOUGH HERE THAT WE'LL BE ABLE TO SEE THE STARS, HUH?

YOU BECOME RESPONSIBLE, FOREVER...

FOR WHAT YOU HAVE TAMED.

THUNK

CRASH—

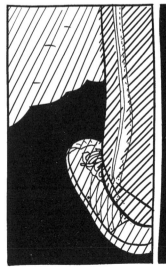

YOU MUST BE HUNGRY!

LET'S HURRY AND EAT BEFORE IT GETS COLD. AH—I'M SO HUNGRY.

IT'S SEAWEED BROTH AND KIMCHI PANCAKES. I MIXED IN THE LEFTOVER KIMCHI BRINE AND PICKLED BITS.

. . . . .

HOW IS THE SEAWEED BROTH?

NEEDS MORE SALT...

WAS YOUR TRIP TO THE SCHOOL OKAY?

YES...

RIIIP

...WHAT ARE YOU GOING TO DO ABOUT TUITION?

I CAN EITHER TRY TO MOVE UP THE BOOK FEES TO COINCIDE WITH REGISTRATION, OR IF THAT DOESN'T WORK, THERE ARE ALWAYS STUDENT LOANS...

~GLUG ~GLUG

I'LL HAVE TO LOOK INTO IT.

YOU'RE DONE?

I'M FULL.

!

YOU HAVEN'T DRAWN THE CURTAINS YET? WHAT IF SOMEONE IS WATCHING US FROM OUTSIDE?!

WHIP

I FORGOT.

...WHAT ARE YOU DOING?

I'M JUST SITTING.

ARE YOU TAKING A BREAK FROM WORKING TODAY?

WELL, I'M TIRED.

THEN...

WOULD YOU TAKE A LOOK AT MY WORK?

. . . .

IT'S ALL DONE.

OH!

WHEW...

....

WELL, THE COMPOSITION DOESN'T ALWAYS WORK.

AND THE COLORS ARE A BIT...

THIS ONE IS KIND OF... AND THE NEXT ONE...

FLIP

....

OVERALL, IT'S GOOD.

REALLY?!

WOO HOO

WOO HOO

EVEN THOUGH YOU NEVER WENT TO SCHOOL FOR ART, YOU'VE GOT A KNACK FOR THIS.

BUT...

IN MY OPINION, YOU NEED TO FIX SOME THINGS...

FOR EXAMPLE, HERE, HERE, AND RIGHT HERE TOO.

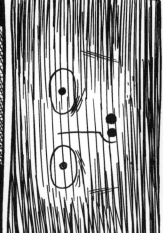

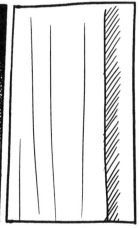

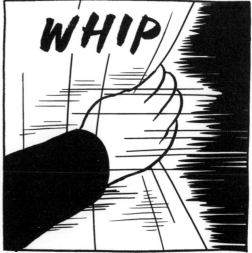

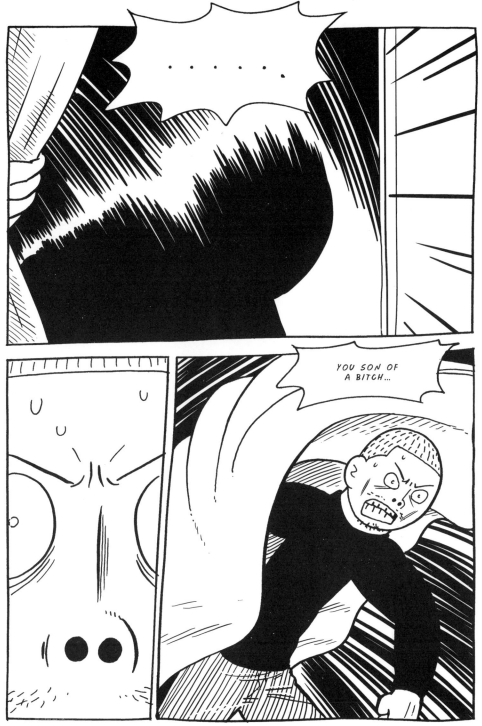

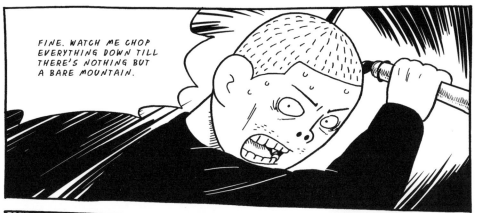

FINE. WATCH ME CHOP EVERYTHING DOWN TILL THERE'S NOTHING BUT A BARE MOUNTAIN.

RIP

TEAR

SLICE TEAR

HACK

STRETCH

PANT PANT

PANT

PANT

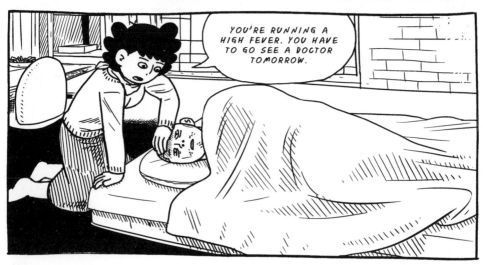

YOU'RE RUNNING A HIGH FEVER. YOU HAVE TO GO SEE A DOCTOR TOMORROW.

HAHH...

GIVE ME SOME-
THING TO CHANGE
INTO, HONEY.

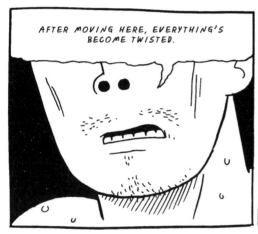

AFTER MOVING HERE, EVERYTHING'S
BECOME TWISTED.

DON'T YOU
THINK SO?

I DON'T
KNOW...

I'M TELLING YOU, THE
CHILL ON THIS MOUNTAIN
IS TOO STRONG. IT'S
DRAINING MY SPIRIT.

· · · · ?

I CAN'T KEEP UP WITH
THE WORLD AS IT SPINS
TO ITS OWN BEAT. WHAT
CAN I DO ABOUT THE
TIME SPENT IDLING ON
THIS MOUNTAIN?

SO WE MOVE BACK TO THE CITY AND LIVE FEROCIOUSLY, SURROUNDED BY PEOPLE!

BUT IF WE LIVE LIKE THAT, TOSSED AROUND BY HARDSHIPS—

WOULDN'T YOU BE ABLE TO RELEASE NEW WORKS EFFORTLESSLY IN THE CITY?

...YOU MAKE A PERSUASIVE ARGUMENT.

SO DON'T THINK ABOUT IT; JUST CLEAR OUT OF HERE...

YOU KNOW WHAT WILL HAPPEN IF YOU KEEP ROTTING AWAY HERE?

YOU'LL DIE!

· · · · · · · · ·

THAT'S RIGHT.

HONEY, YOUR CLOTHES...

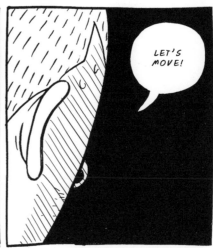

LET'S MOVE!

I CAN'T TAKE IT ANYMORE...

GO SEE A DOCTOR FIRST.

열린 의원

LET'S PICK UP YOUR MEDICINE, EAT SOMETHING WARM, AND THEN GO HOME.

WITH WHAT MONEY...?

COUGH

...I BORROWED IT FROM A FRIEND. WHEN YOUR PAYCHECK COMES IN, WE HAVE TO PAY HER BACK.

WHERE ARE YOU GOING?

FOR A WALK...

I'M COMING WITH YOU.

PANT PANT

MEOOOOW

MEOW

WHY...WHY...
WHY...

WHY WON'T THIS ANGER IN
MY HEART LEAVE ME...

IS THIS WHAT I WANT?

· · · · ·

...WHY?

HONEY...
LOOK OVER
THERE...

OUR
SMALL
HOUSE...

OUR SECLUDED HOUSE, DEEP
IN THE MOUNTAIN...

...BECAUSE I HATE THE CITY?
...BECAUSE I HAVE NO MONEY?

WHAT DO WE DO
NOW, HONEY?

HOW...HOW ARE
WE GOING TO LIVE
FROM NOW ON...?

IT WAS URGENT, SO I BORROWED MONEY FOR NOW, BUT... AFTER THIS...

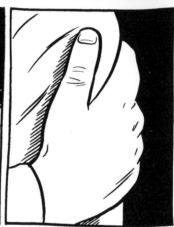

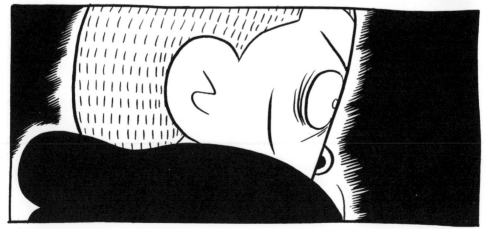

WE LIVE
HERE—!!

I SAID, WE
LIVE HERE—!!

HEY
NOW, HEY
NOW.

IT'S A LONG TIME
BEFORE THE END OF
HIBERNATION. ARE
YOU GOING TO KEEP
MAKING SO MUCH
NOISE SHAKING THE
FROZEN GROUND?

WAAAAAAA AAAH

GURGLE

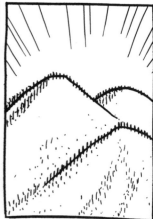

266

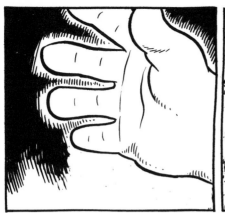

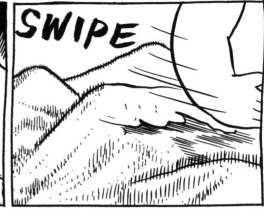

NNNG...

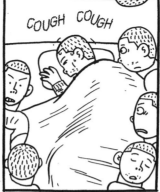

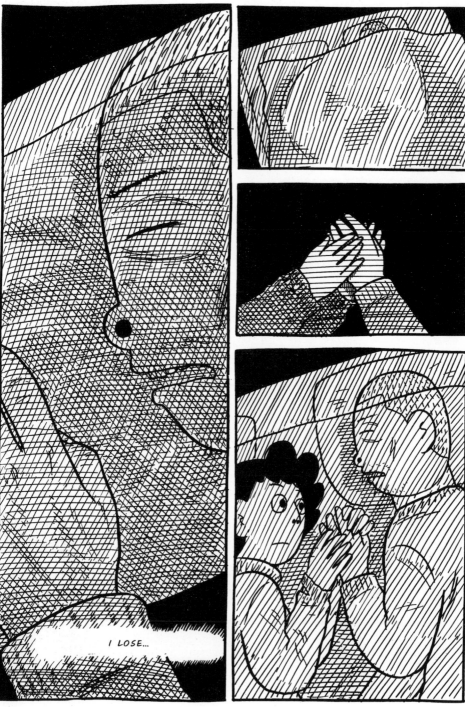

I LOSE...

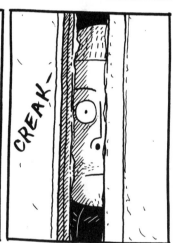

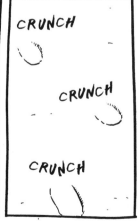

I NEVER REALIZED...

THAT SUCH BEAUTIFUL
SNOW EXISTED SO
CLOSE TO HOME...

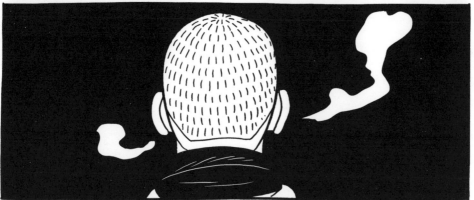

DAMN.

THE MOUNTAIN IS STILL HERE, UNCHANGED...

JUST WHAT HAVE I SEEN, AND WHAT HAVE I TRIED NOT TO SEE ON THIS MOUNTAIN...?

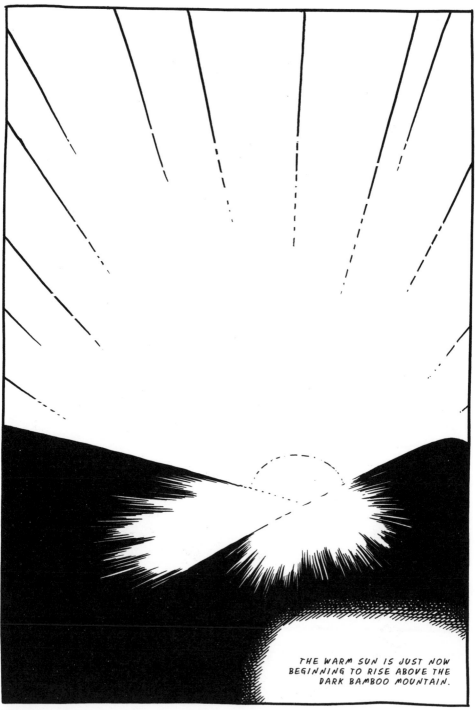

THE WARM SUN IS JUST NOW
BEGINNING TO RISE ABOVE THE
DARK BAMBOO MOUNTAIN.

Winter Part 4

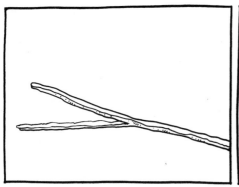
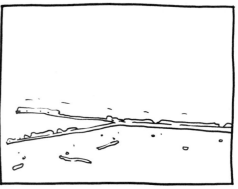

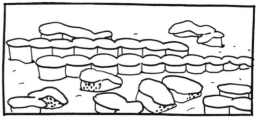

THERE'S NO ONE UP HERE, SO LET'S LET HIM FROLIC TO HIS HEART'S CONTENT.

TING

GET AWAY! YOU'LL GET DIRT ON ME!

PANT
PANT
♪
PANT

HEY—BUT WE'RE GOING UP THE MOUNTAIN.

LET'S GO. HE CAN FOLLOW US OR NOT.

...

DID WE UNLEASH HIM FOR NOTHING?

ZOOM

HEY YOU LITTLE—STOP RIGHT THERE!!!

♪

I WAS RE-ALLY FOND OF THAT LEATHER GLOVE...

HUU- HUU- HUU-

HONEY, WAIT FOR ME!

OH YEAH!

WHAT ABOUT YOUR GLOVE?

HE'S TOO FAST, SO...

MEOW

IT'S BEEN SO LONG SINCE WE WALKED UP HERE.

MEOW

CRUNCH

CRUNCH

CRUNCH

THERE'S NO PLACE LIKE SNOW COUNTRY!

IT'S SO CHARMING.

HONEY...

HMM?

AFTER SUCH A HARD WINTER, YOU LOOK MUCH BRIGHTER THESE DAYS.

YOU MIGHT SAY I LET GO OF SOMETHING I WAS STRUGGLING TO HOLD ON TO.

?

I WAS SO SICK THAT I LOST ABOUT FIFTEEN POUNDS IN A MONTH... I'M JUST GLAD I GOT BETTER.

YAP!

IT'S A SOUVENIR!

UGH!

PAF

I'M SO RELIEVED YOU'VE CHEERED UP—

WINTER STILL ISN'T OVER—

BUT LET'S ENJOY IT—

LALALALA—

LALALA

ENJOY THAT COLD
AND FRESH AIR—

EVEN THOUGH SPRING
IS WARM—

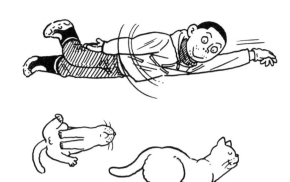

WINTER IS SUCH A
LOVELY SEASON—

HAVE A
GOOD TRIP.

TO
GWANGNEUNG...

I'M LEFT ALONE WHILE MY WIFE MAKES THE LONG TRIP TO PAJU PUBLISHING, WHERE SHE HAS A MEETING TO GO OVER SOME MANUSCRIPT PAGES.

THE STORY IS GOOD, SO WE'D LIKE TO OFFER YOU A CONTRACT FOR THE WRITING ONLY!

SIGNS: PHRENOLOGY; FORTUNE TELLING

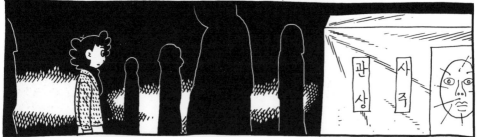

FLASH

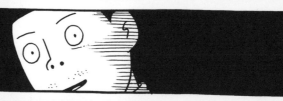

VROOM

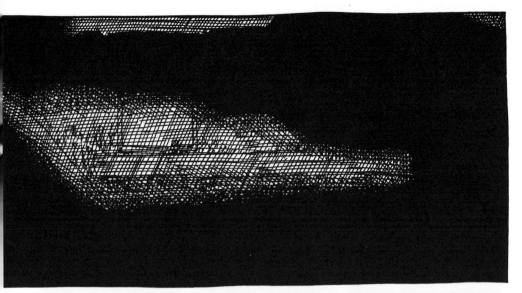

THE PUBLISHER'S IDEAS WERE REALLY DIFFERENT FROM MINE, SO I NEED TO THINK ABOUT IT SOME MORE.

...OF COURSE. YOU SHOULD TAKE YOUR TIME.

I MIGHT REFINE IT SOME MORE TO PREPARE FOR THE COMPETITION.

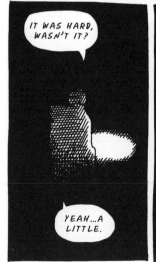

IT WAS HARD, WASN'T IT?

YEAH...A LITTLE.

OH, YEAH! I SAW A FORTUNE-TELLER, AND HE SAID IT WOULD ALL BE RESOLVED AFTER APRIL.

A FORTUNE-TELLER! PFFF!

ANYWAY, IT MADE ME FEEL BETTER.

CREAK

CR-
CR-
CREAK

CRACK

OH MAN, IF IT GETS ANY COLDER, THE DOOR'S GONNA FREEZE SHUT.

SQUEAK

BREAKFAST TIME—

RUSTLE

SHAKE SHAKE

NO ONE COMES UP THE MOUNTAIN NOW.

WHEN THE WEATHER'S GOOD, EVERYONE COMES UP TO SEE THE MOUNTAIN CHANGE ITS CLOTHES, BUT NOW THAT IT'S COLD, THEY DON'T COME AROUND...

THOSE ALPINE CLUB MEMBERS NEVER MISS A CHANCE TO COME UP HERE IN THE SPRING AND SUMMER TO TIE RIBBONS AROUND EVERY BRANCH IN THE FOREST, BUT HOW CAN THEY NEGLECT TO VISIT NOW, TO WITNESS THIS SCENERY...

HOW IS IT SO NICE AND QUIET HERE?

HE'S COME UP HERE TODAY TOO...

WOW

STARTLE

YOU WERE SEARCHING FOR CARS ON THE INTERNET AGAIN, WEREN'T YOU?

WE'VE GOT TO GATHER INFORMATION AHEAD OF TIME SO WHEN WE CAN ACTUALLY AFFORD A CAR, WE'RE READY!

CLICK

LATELY, HONEY, WHEN YOU SHOULD BE WORKING, YOU GO ON THE INTERNET INSTEAD...

WHEN YOU'RE EXAMINING THE STATE OF THE REVOLVING WORLD FROM UP ON A MOUNTAIN, A COUPLE HOURS REALLY JUST...

THAT'S AN EXCUSE! YOU WEAR OUT THE THROTTLE BY LOOKING AT AUCTION, CAR, AND CAMERA SITES.

IF YOU'RE THAT CURIOUS ABOUT WORLDLY AFFAIRS, YOU SHOULD SUBSCRIBE TO A NEWSPAPER!

AH! WHAT DID YOU SAY?!

IN AN AGE WHERE NEWS ARTICLES ARE UPDATED INSTANTLY, WHY SO PRIMITIVE...?!

HELLO, IS THIS XX NEWSPAPER DEPOT? OUR ADDRESS IS ***, AND IF YOU'D START THE SUBSCRIPTION TOMORROW...

OH YEAH, AND HOW LONG DOES THE FREE TRIAL SUBSCRIPTION LAST? WHAT? ONLY A MONTH?

IN THE CITY, THEY GIVE YOU FREE GIFTS LIKE BIKES AND WHATNOT WHEN YOU SUBSCRIBE. THEY REALLY CLENCH THOSE PURSE STRINGS HERE!!

WHY ARE NEWSPAPERS GIVING YOU THAT KIND OF STUFF IN THE FIRST PLACE?

ANYWAY, THEY SAID THEY'D BE DELIVERING THE NEWSPAPER TO THE MAILBOX WAAAAY DOWN BY THE MOUNTAIN ENTRANCE.

WHAT DID YOU SAY?

THEY SAID SOMETHING OR OTHER ABOUT HOW THEIR MOTORCYCLES CAN'T DRIVE UP THE FROZEN ROAD THROUGH SNOW.

WHAT'S WRONG WITH THIS NEIGHBORHOOD'S NEWSPAPER DELIVERY?!

CHEW
CHEW

NOM
NOM

WE'RE NEARLY OUT OF CAT FOOD. LET'S BUY A TWENTY POUND BAG OF RICE, AND THEN USE THE LEFTOVER MONEY TO BUY FOOD FOR THE ANIMALS.

BUT...

SMACK... SMACK...

EATING NOTHING BUT KIMCHI EVERY DAY IS MAKING MY INSIDES SOUR.

HOW ABOUT YOU?

MMM...SOONER OR LATER WE'LL HAVE TO GET GROCERIES TOO...

LET'S GO WITH THE TEN POUND BAG OF RICE, THEN SPEND WHAT'S LEFT ON SOME OTHER FOOD.

CLATTER

CLATTER

PFUU

PFUU

SCRAPE
SCRAPE

SCRAPE

I STOPPED WASHING MY FACE FOR FOUR DAYS, JUST BECAUSE I HAD NO PLANS TO SEE ANYONE... I OVERDID IT.

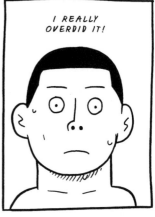

HUH? LOOK AT MY BELLY!

I REALLY OVERDID IT!

HONEY, THE PHONE!

PUBLISHER.

...OKAY!

. . . .

YES...YES... THE SERVER? OKAY.

OKAY, KEEP UP THE GOOD WORK.

THEY MUST HAVE OKAYED YOUR DRAWINGS!

THEY SAID THEY UPLOADED A LIST OF CORRECTIONS TO THE WEB SERVER.

YAWN~

THIS WAY IS ORGANIZED. I LIKE IT.

DRIP
DRIP

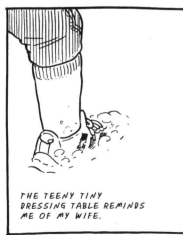

THE TEENY TINY
DRESSING TABLE REMINDS
ME OF MY WIFE.

BORN IN
WINTER
BEAUTIFUL
YOU—*

MEOOOOOOOW

SONG: "WINTER CHILD," (1980) LEE JONG-YONG'S HIT BALLAD

I'M NO DIFFERENT THAN MY WIFE.

KVRK

KVRRRK

CLEAN LIKE THE SNOW...

MY OWN DARLING—

BUT SPRING, SUMMER, FALL, AND WINTER—

KVRK

KVRRRK

KVRK

I WISH MY WIFE WEREN'T SO NAÏVE.

BUT SHE IS.

WHEW—

ALWAYS... WHEW—

KVRRRK-

KVRK

CLEAR...HUFF...

KVRRRK

SHE BECAME NAÏVE WHEN SHE BECAME MY WIFE.

OOF-

OOF-
OOF-

CRACK

...I WASN'T ABLE TO GIVE HER THE SPACE TO MAKE ANOTHER CHOICE.

CR-CR-CR-CR-CRACK

CRK

CRK

CRRREAAAACK

2006년
○○○○상 공모

THE DEADLINE
IS MARCH 31...AND
IT'S ALREADY
FEBRUARY 12...

SKREEEE

EPSON
GT700

SCREEN: 2006 AWARDS COMPETITION

THE INDIVIDUAL WHO SAID HE'D TAKE A SHORT WALK IS QUITE LATE.

HONEY, WHERE ARE YOU? I'M HUNGRY.

I'M ON MY WAY UP. SOAK THE RICE.

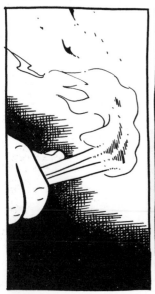

I ADDED UP A FEW ACCOUNT BALANCES, AND THEY CAME OUT TO ABOUT ₩20,000, SO I BOUGHT A FEW THINGS.

BEAN SPROUTS, TOFU, POTATOES, EGGS, FISH CAKES, SQUASH, GARLIC, GREEN ONIONS, LETTUCE, PEPPERS, AND IN THE END, THE PORK WAS ON SALE, SO...

'TSSSSS

. . . .

TSSSSS

TSSSSSSS

TSSS

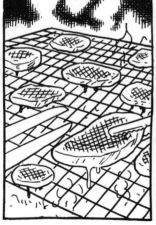

SAY AHHH—

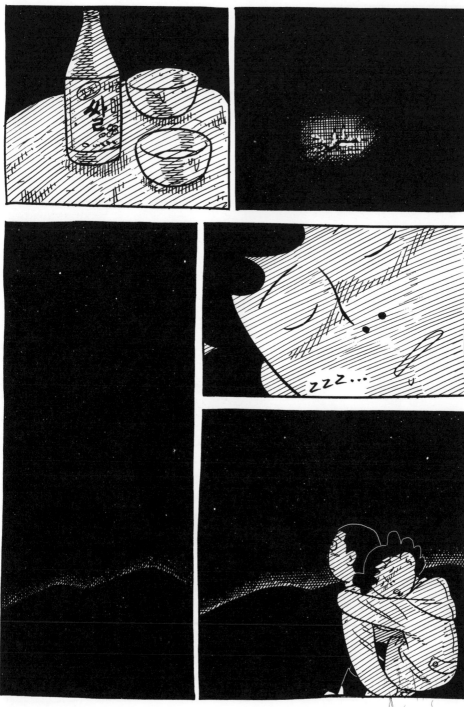

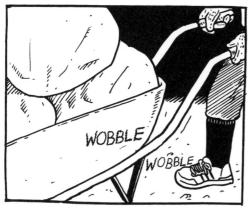

OH!

HAVE YOU BEEN WELL?!

OH MY! OH MY GOODNESS...

WHAT HAPPENED? DIDN'T SEE HIDE NOR HAIR O' Y'ALL. I THOUGHT YOU COULDN'T DEAL, SO YOU'D MOVED AWAY. HOWZIT? AIN'T IT SCARY? HOW CAN YOU LIVE UP IN THAT THERE MOUNTAIN? IF IT WERE ME, I WOULDN'T BE ABLE TO LIVE UP THERE, IT BEING SO SCARY AND ALL.

CHAT CHIT CHIT CHAT CHAT CHAT CHIT CHAT

WHERE'S THE MISSUS? YOU'RE BOTH JUST THE SAME. HOW DO Y'ALL LOOK SO ALIKE?

AH, YES...

WELL Y'ALL SURE ARE BRAVE!

HEH HEH HEH

GO 'BOUTCHER BUSINESS.

IT'S ALREADY MID-FEBRUARY, BUT MY HEART CAN'T DECIDE.

SCREEN: ENROLLMENT

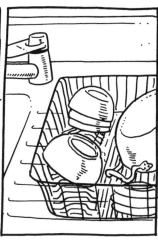

WEED THE FIELD WITH ME, HONEY.

WHAT ARE YOU TALKING ABOUT? THIS EARLY IN THE YEAR!?

WE HAVE TO PREPARE THE SOIL AHEAD OF TIME!

AND WHAT TRICK WILL YOU USE TO TURN OVER FROZEN DIRT?

IF YOU DON'T WANT TO HELP, FORGET IT.

GIMME A BREAK.

YOU WANT ME TO DITCH THE WORK I NEED TO FINISH TO HELP YOU WEED A FIELD IN THE DEAD OF WINTER? DOES THAT MAKE ANY SENSE?

SCRITCH SCRATCH

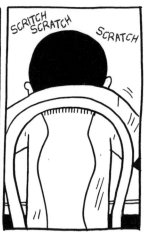

SCRITCH SCRATCH

SCRATCH

SCRATCH SCRATCH

TAK

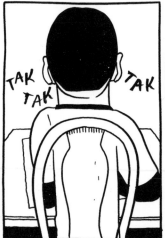

TAK
TAK

TAK

ARE YOU KIDDING ME?!

TAK

TAK

TAK

TAK

AHEM—

OUT OF THE WAY.

BUT YOUR MANUSCRIPT...

IT'S BREAK TIME.

YOU'RE GOING TO BE STRESSED IF YOU GET ANOTHER FRANTIC CALL FROM YOUR EDITOR. GO INSIDE AND WORK.

TAK TAK

UGH, C'MON. MOVE IT!

AH!

BIFF

STOP PECK- IN', YA HEN.

HOW DO YOU EXPECT TO FINISH IT ALL IF YOU KEEP PECKIN' AT IT LIKE THAT?

TSK...

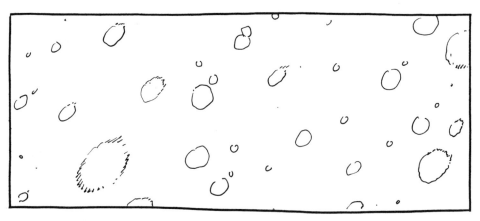

 MONEY FOR TRANS-
PORTATION COSTS,
LET ALONE TUITION,
IS SCARCE...

 EVEN IF IT'S HARD,
WE'RE ADAPTING
TO THIS LIFE.

 BUT IF YOU QUIT SCHOOL
NOW, I KNOW YOU'LL
REGRET IT.

...I KNOW THAT
TOO, BUT...

 HONEY, YOU NEED TO FOCUS ON DOING THE IMPORTANT THINGS
FIRST, BEFORE ALL THE URGENT STRESSFUL TASKS.

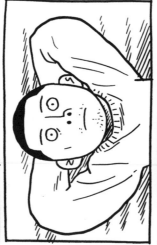

 ZZZ...

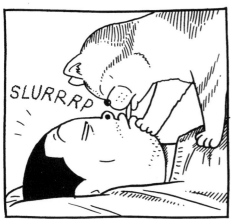

HEY, SO...

DO YOU EVER GET THE FEELING WE'RE JUST PLAYING HOUSE?

WHETHER IT'S YOUR FRIENDS OR MY FRIENDS, SOME LIVE IN APARTMENTS WITH HIGH PROPERTY VALUES, HAVE KIDS, STABLE EMPLOYMENT...

COMPARED TO THEM, IT JUST FEELS LIKE WE'RE LIVING DAY TO DAY.

SHOULDN'T WE BE CONCERNED ABOUT BUILDING A STABLE LIFE SO WE CAN HAVE KIDS?

WELL, IT WOULD BE PRETTY NICE TO HAVE A STEADY MONTHLY INCOME.

...I GUESS SO.

BUT WE'RE US! WE ARE CREATIVE PEOPLE WHO MAKE CREATIVE WORK.

BEING ABLE TO WRITE AND DRAW FOREVER AND EVER TILL WE GROW OLD AND DIE ISN'T A PRIVILEGE THAT'S BESTOWED UPON JUST ANYONE!

AND YOU!

FLINCH

YOU'RE SAYING... I NEED TO WORK HARDER ON MY STORY CONCEPTS?

DO WE HAVE TO HAVE A BABY?

. . . .

WANTING TO PASS ON WHAT WE'VE GAINED FROM THE PREVIOUS GENERATION TO THE NEXT IS A NATURAL DESIRE.

ALSO...

EVEN IF WE MAKE THE PERFECT HOME, WON'T IT FEEL LIKE SOMETHING IS MISSING?

HOW ABOUT I JUST DO TWICE AS MANY SWEET THINGS? I CAN JUST DO CUTE STUFF!

HUH?

HUH?

AH JEEZ!

MARCH IS HERE. THE FIRST OF THE MONTH IS OUR FIRST WEDDING ANNIVERSARY. THAT MEANS TODAY...

I MADE MY WIFE AN ANNIVERSARY CARD. WE ARE VISITING THE FOOT OF THE MOUNTAIN FOR THE FIRST TIME IN A WHILE.

WE TOOK SOUVENIR PHOTOS IN NEARBY BONGSEUNSA AND GWANGNEUNG.

WE EVEN HAD SOME INSTANT RAMEN IN THE PARK.

SLURRP

WHEN YOU COME TO A PLACE LIKE THIS, CUP RAMEN IS THE BEST!

ON OUR FIRST WEDDING ANNIVERSARY, I DREW A CARD AND THRUST IT AT MY WIFE, AND WE WALKED AROUND HOLDING HANDS ALL DAY. I COULDN'T DO ANYTHING ELSE FOR HER.

MY WIFE IS LAUGHING FOR SOME REASON.

HANG ON!

SHE DUSTS OFF HER HUSBAND AND WALKS AROUND WITH HIM LIKE THIS, JUST TO TAKE THE BUS AND BUY SOME RAMEN.

PAF

TAKE THAT!

AND YET, FOR SOME REASON, SHE STILL LAUGHS.

IF I FEEL HAPPINESS, I'M A SHAMELESS HUSBAND.

BUT TODAY I'M HERE JUST TRYING TO BE HAPPY.

I PUSH MY FEELINGS OF GUILT AND SELF-PITY OFF UNTIL TOMORROW. JUST FOR TODAY, I'LL BE SHAMELESS.

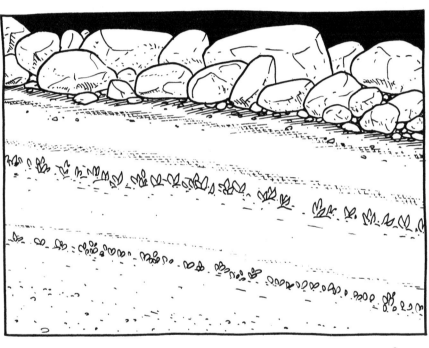

Spring

"DEPTH OF FIELD" REFERS TO THE DEPTH OF THE FOCUS.

IN OTHER WORDS, THE FOCUS FITS THE AREA.

SQUEEEEK

OH MAN, LATE AGAIN.

SCHOOL SURE IS FAR FROM POCHEON...

YO—!

HAVE YOU HAD LUNCH?

NAH, I'VE GOT A BIT OF A STOMACHACHE.

239

GO AND EAT WITHOUT ME.

OKAY...

GRRRUUUMBLE

MY WIFE MUST BE PREPARING LUNCH RIGHT ABOUT NOW, HUH...? I WONDER WHAT SHE'S EATING...

SIDE DISH!

PLUCK

OUR CELL PHONE SERVICE HAS BEEN DIS-CONNECTED, SO I CAN'T EVEN CALL HER...

MY PAYCHECK IS SUPPOSED TO COME IN AT THE END OF THE MONTH, BUT UNTIL THEN...

CELL PHONE, LANDLINE, INTERNET...WE CAN'T USE ANY OF IT...

HWEEEEEEEEE

HWOOOOOOOOOOO

HOOOOOOOO~

CH-CH-CH-CH-CHK

KA-THUMP

SCREECH

TONIGHT'S WIND IS MAKING QUITE A COMMOTION.

SCARY~

SHF

HWOOO

SCRITCH SCRATCH

YAWN

HWEEEEE-

HWEEEEEEEEEEE-

SESAME SEEDS, LETTUCE, CUCUMBERS, MUGWORT, SQUASH, PEAS, CORN...

WE'LL ORDER THESE FOR NOW, AND BUY THE REST AS SEEDLINGS LATER.

SEEDLINGS ARE THE ONES WITH NEW SHOOTS, RIGHT?

WHAT SHALL WE HAVE FOR DINNER?

CLICK

홍지훈

모디아
문서
바이크
자동차

"A WISE CHOICE, GIVEN HIGH OIL PRICES. GOOD CARS LIKE THIS DON'T WAIT. GUARANTEED NO ACCIDENTS. LOOKING TO EXCHANGE FOR A SIMILAR USED CAR."

GULP

SCREEN: BOOKMARKS/DOCUMENTS/MOTORCYCLES/CARS

CLANG

CLANG

CLANG

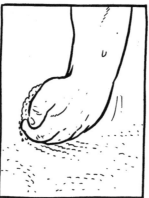

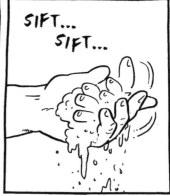

SIFT...
SIFT...

THE DIRT'S BECOME SOFTER...

THE CROPS WILL GROW BETTER.

WHEN MY WIFE WAS YOUNG, SHE TRIED HER HAND AT GARDENING, SO SHE KNOWS MORE ABOUT IT THAN THIS CITY BOY.

GOOD WORK TODAY.

YOW...MY JOINTS.

I'LL JUST LIE DOWN FOR A SECOND, THEN GET UP AND DO SOME WORK.

342

SHK
SHK

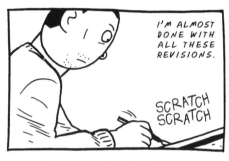

I'M ALMOST DONE WITH ALL THESE REVISIONS.

SCRATCH
SCRATCH

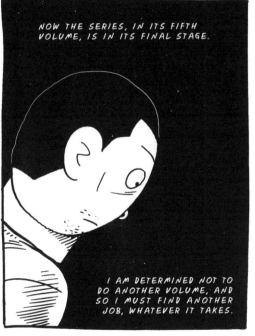

NOW THE SERIES, IN ITS FIFTH VOLUME, IS IN ITS FINAL STAGE.

I AM DETERMINED NOT TO DO ANOTHER VOLUME, AND SO I MUST FIND ANOTHER JOB, WHATEVER IT TAKES.

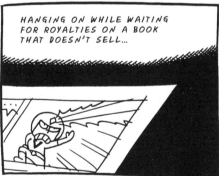

HANGING ON WHILE WAITING FOR ROYALTIES ON A BOOK THAT DOESN'T SELL...

ink

THIS IS WHERE IT ENDS...

343

POK
POK

POK
POK

HESITATE

WRIGGLE~

HEY THERE— WATCH WHERE YOU'RE DIGGING!

YOU ALMOST SLICED ME TO PIECES!

BE CAREFUL FROM NOW ON, MMF MMF.

ALL RIGHT, ALL RIGHT! JEEZ ALREADY.

OOF—MY BACK.

SINCE I CLEARED OUT MOST OF THE BIG ROCKS YESTERDAY...

IF I TURN OVER THIS MUCH DIRT EACH MORNING...

AND I PICK OUT THE SMALL ROCKS TOO...

VROOM...

HONEY!!
BREAKFAST!!

WHEN DID YOU
WAKE UP?

SEVEN
O'CLOCK?

IF I TILL THE GROUND
FOR A COUPLE HOURS
EACH MORNING, WE
MIGHT BE ABLE TO PLANT
SOME SEEDS BY THE DAY
AFTER TOMORROW.

WE COULD EVEN FER-
TILIZE THE SOIL WITH
SOME DOG AND CAT
POOP LATER TODAY.

NO, IT'S FINE.
THAT'S ENOUGH
FOR TODAY!

IF YOU WANT
TO, GO AHEAD.

YOU SHOULD
HAVE WOKEN
ME UP.

INSTEAD OF
DOING IT ALL
YOURSELF.

I COULD WAKE YOU UP, BUT WHY IS THAT MY JOB?

WHAT?

WHAT IF YOU DON'T GET UP WHEN I WAKE YOU? WHAT AM I SUPPOSED TO DO ABOUT IT?

EH, I'LL WAKE YOU UP TOMORROW; GET UP OR DON'T.

WHAT'S WITH YOU?

INSTEAD OF GETTING ANGRY THAT I DIDN'T WAKE YOU UP, YOU SHOULD ASK YOURSELF WHY YOU BLAME SOMEONE ELSE FOR NOT BEING ABLE TO GET UP IN THE MORNING.

I GET THAT YOU NEED LOTS OF SLEEP, BUT I DON'T FEEL LIKE BEING RESPONSIBLE FOR ANY OF THIS. LET'S JUST STOP TALKING ABOUT IT.

WHEN I WAS YOUNG, WE LIVED IN A HOUSEHOLD THAT WOKE UP AT DAWN EVERY DAY TO SAY GOODBYE TO OUR FATHER.

HAVE A GOOD DAY, FATHER!

WE'D EAT BREAKFAST AT DAWN...

AND ARRIVE AT SCHOOL JUST AFTER.

HEY, MISTER, LET ME IN...

DING-DING-A-LING-A-LING TOFU FOR SALE-

I DIDN'T WANT TO FORCE MY WIFE, WHO HAS BEEN SLEEPY SINCE CHILDHOOD, TO MAKE BREAKFAST FOR ME JUST BECAUSE WE HAD GOTTEN MARRIED.

AHH—GOOD MORNING. I'M HUNGRY!

WHILE WE STRUGGLED FOR A LONG TIME TO TRY AND WAKE UP TOGETHER, IT WAS BETTER FOR MY MENTAL HEALTH TO GIVE UP AND TRY TO RESPECT HER WAKE UP TIME.

ZZZ...

ZZZ...

AND A HUNGRY PERSON CAN FEED HIMSELF JUST FINE.

... YAWN

THE WAY I LOOK AT IT, ON MORNINGS LIKE THESE, I'M RESPONSIBLE FOR COOKING WHATEVER GOES IN MY MOUTH.

MY COOKING HOBBY HAS DEFINITELY SOLVED MY NEED FOR OTHERS TO COOK FOR ME...YOU COULD ALSO SAY I'VE ADOPTED THAT HOBBY DUE TO MY INNATE DESIRE FOR FOOD...

BURRRP

IT JUST SEEMS PROBLEMATIC IF YOU BLAME SOMEONE ELSE FOR YOU NOT HAVING THE WILL TO WAKE YOURSELF UP IN THE MORNINGS!

NYEH!

WAIT, DON'T YOU HAVE CLASS TODAY?!

I'VE GOT SOME THINGS I REALLY NEED TO DEAL WITH, SO I CAN'T GO.

...REALLY?

THUD

WE'RE NEARLY OUT OF MONEY, AND THE BUS FARE ALONE WOULD BREAK THE BANK...

THE COAL IS PROBABLY GOING TO RUN OUT TOMORROW.

WHAT ARE WE GOING TO DO? WE STILL NEED TO HEAT THE HOUSE...

AND YOU NEED TO PAY YOUR TUITION...

EH, DON'T WORRY ABOUT TUITION. WE'LL FIGURE SOMETHING OUT BEFORE THE END OF NEXT MONTH.

₩350...IF WE USE SEVEN BRIQUETTES A DAY, THAT'S ₩2,450...TO HEAT THE HOUSE THROUGH APRIL, THAT'S FORTY-FIVE DAYS TIMES ₩2,450, WHICH COMES TO ₩110,250...

349

AH—
CHOO

UGH, IT'S COLD—

IT'S BEEN TWENTY MINUTES...

IT'S HERE!

WHEW...I'M GLAD I GOT A SEAT...

!...

AM I ON THE WRONG BUS?!

SQUEAK

VROOM—

IT'S WILD WASABI!!

HERE TOO...!

THIS FIELD IS A WASABI GOLDMINE!

WOO HOO!

IS IT REALLY WASABI...?

SNIFF

SNIFF

SNIFF

IT IS!!!

LET'S PICK SOME HERBS ON THE MOUNTAIN WHILE WE'RE AT IT.

PLUCK

PLUCK

PLUCK

354

WHEN WAS THAT COMPETITION DEADLINE AGAIN?

TOMORROW.

SLURP...

SLURP...

THE APPLICATION FEE IS ₩30,000.

SHOULD I JUST KEEP WORKING ON IT AND TAKE IT TO A PUBLISHER?

THE APPLICATION FEE IS EXPENSIVE.

...DO YOU HAVE THE MONEY?

I DO, IN SAVINGS!

BUT I THINK I WANT TO REFINE MY WORK A BIT AND TAKE IT TO A DIFFERENT PUBLISHER. PAYING TO ENTER A COMPETITION IS JUST...

....

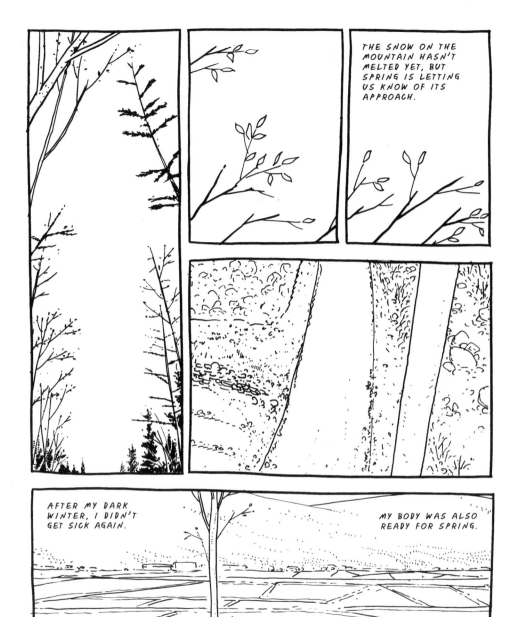

THE SNOW ON THE MOUNTAIN HASN'T MELTED YET, BUT SPRING IS LETTING US KNOW OF ITS APPROACH.

AFTER MY DARK WINTER, I DIDN'T GET SICK AGAIN.

MY BODY WAS ALSO READY FOR SPRING.

HERE...

SO THE COMPETITION FEE WAS PAID FOR WITH MY WIFE'S SAVINGS.

OPEN

SHUT

VROOOM...

MY MOM LOANED US THE MONEY.

...YOU DIDN'T ASK HER, DID YOU...

NO. THEY RECEIVED A RETURN ON THEIR INSURANCE POLICY. SHE SAID THEY DIDN'T NEED IT RIGHT NOW...

WHEN YOU GET YOUR NEXT PAYCHECK, WE HAVE TO PAY HER BACK, OKAY?

OF COURSE...

HEY! THERE'S SOMETHING I WANT TO EAT, SO LET'S GO BUY IT.

HUH? OKAY.

TAXI!

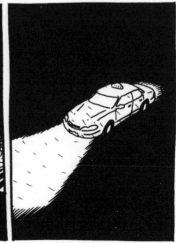

HM, I'VE NEVER SEEN THIS CAB DRIVER BEFORE.

YOU CAN DROP US OFF IN FRONT OF THE OAK TREE REST AREA.

WHERE DO YOU LIVE?

IT'S UP AT THE TOP OF THE MOUNTAIN, SO WE CAN JUST WALK FROM—

OH, I'LL JUST DRIVE UP TO YOUR HOUSE THEN.

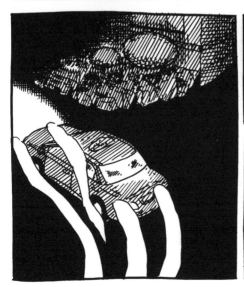

데생

　1화 데생
　1화 데생 수정 1차
　1화 데생 수정 2차
　1화 데생 수정 3차
　　1화 데생 수정 4차
　2화 데생
　2화 데생 수정 1차
　2화 데생 수정 2차
　2화 데생 수정 3차
　3화 데생 수정 1차

TEXT: LONG LIST OF REVISIONS

11화 데생
11화 데생 수정 1차
11화 데생 수정 2차
11화 데생 수정 3차
1 화 데생 수정 4차
12화 데생
　화 데생 수정 1차
　화 데생 수정 2차
　화 데생 수정 3차
. . .

THESE ARE BRUISES OF GLORY.

I THINK I NEED TO END WITH THIS VOLUME.

BUT WHY NOW? YOU'VE KEPT UP A GOOD PACE LATELY.

THE WORK IS HARD, AND LIVING IS HARD TOO. I'M SORRY.

YOU SHOULD HOLD ON A BIT LONGER. THERE MIGHT BE ANOTHER ROYALTY CHECK COMING IN THIS MONTH.

WHAT? REALLY?!!

THAT'S WHAT I SAID!

HONEY?

FROM NOW ON, ALL ANTAGONISTIC ASSHOLES—

BOOM

—GET BEAT DOWN!

...THAT'S WHAT YOU'RE THINKING WHEN YOU GO HIKING THESE DAYS?

I'M JUST RE-LEASING STRESS. IT DOESN'T MEAN ANYTHING.

IF YOU'RE BRIMMING WITH THAT MUCH ENERGY, LET'S FORAGE FOR SOME MUGWORT LATER.

DON'T PRESS THE DIRT; JUST COVER THE SEED LIGHTLY.

LIKE THIS?

*RICE MIXED WITH GREENS, MEAT, AND RED PEPPER PASTE

I JUST PASSED OUT...

HONEY, WAKE UP. WE HAVE TO EAT DINNER.

OHHH— MY JOINTS—

HNNG

COLD

UGH, WE OVERDID IT!

CLICK

HONEY, GIVE ME A BLANKET...

CUCKOO— CUCKOO—

CHIRP CHIRP

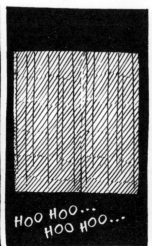

HOO HOO... HOO HOO...

PIIII...

NOW THAT IT'S SPRING, THE BIRD CALLS HAVE REALLY CHANGED.

PIIII...

BLANKEEET!

373

SIGN: WE OPPOSE BUILDING A MORTUARY BY THE SCHOOL

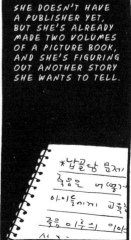

375

AWWWWWW—I WANNA WORK ON MY OWN STUFF TOO.

PLAN OUT A STORY WHENEVER YOU'VE GOT A MINUTE. WHAT GOOD IS IT JUST THINKING ABOUT IT?

BUT THERE ARE SO MANY CHORES AROUND THE HOUSE, AND THE GARDEN TOO.

SNOOP

!

YOU SAID YOU WERE SCANNING YOUR WORK, BUT YOU'VE BEEN LOOKING AT THIS!

I'VE FINISHED SCANNING, AND I WAS JUST TAKING A QUICK BREAK, WIFE.

SMACK

WE'RE STILL NOT IN ANY POSITION TO BUY A CAR!

EVEN IF IT'S NOT RIGHT AWAY...

NO. WAY.

376

BUT WHEN I THINK ABOUT THE CONFLICT BETWEEN THE EDITORIAL STAFF AND ME, IN MY EFFORTS TO BE WITHOUT DEBT...

YOU'VE FINALLY FINISHED!

YES, THANK YOU FOR ALL YOUR HARD WORK ALONG THE WAY.

I REALIZE THAT I CAN'T BE A PART OF THAT KIND OF CONFLICT AGAIN.

IT'S A PITY TO END THINGS HERE.

BUT THAT'S HOW IT GOES...

SO I'VE LEARNED SOMETHING AFTER ALL.

IT MUST HAVE BEEN DIFFICULT TO DEAL WITH SUCH A TROUBLE-MAKER LIKE ME.

HA HAHA

SO YOU'RE REALLY NOT WORKING ON THE NEXT VOLUME?

NO. ANOTHER WOULD BE TOO DIFFICULT.

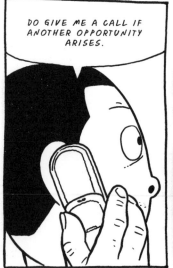

DO GIVE ME A CALL IF ANOTHER OPPORTUNITY ARISES.

WHY WOULD I CALL AN ARTIST WHO'S LEAVING BECAUSE HE DOESN'T WANT TO WORK ANYMORE?

IF YOU DON'T TAKE CARE OF ME, YOU MIGHT REGRET IT!

HMPH, NO THANK YOU!

WHIP

RIBBON: HISTORICAL SOCIETY

MY WIFE AND I
LIVE ON THIS
MOUNTAIN.

SO THE OWNERS OF THIS MOUNTAIN ARE US.

WHEN YOU LIVE IN THE CITY, YOU'RE NOT CONCERNED WITH WHAT GOES ON OUTSIDE YOUR FRONT DOOR.

BUT WHEN YOU LIVE IN THE COUNTRY, YOU'RE NOT CONCERNED WITH WHAT GOES ON OUTSIDE THE VILLAGE.

FROM NOW ON...

I'M NOT CONCERNED WITH WHAT GOES ON OUTSIDE THIS MOUNTAIN.

THEREFORE ...

WHAT DO YOU THINK YOU'RE DOING, MISTER—?!

WHO DO YOU THINK'S GONNA PICK UP AFTER YOU?!

HEY, JUST PICK IT UP AND LET'S GO.

SO I MUST GET INVOLVED IN THIS MOUNTAIN'S AFFAIRS!

LET'S GO INSIDE.

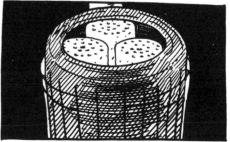

THANKS TO YOU, WE SURVIVED THE WINTER! WE SHOULD GIVE YOU AN ACHIEVEMENT AWARD, AT LEAST!

TRUER WORDS!

YOU GAVE US HOT WATER!

AND YOU DRIED OUR LAUNDRY.

YOU GRILLED FISH JERKY FOR US! AND SEAWEED AND MACKEREL!

YOU EVEN SIMMERED CHICKEN SOUP FOR US!

YOU THINK THAT'S ALL? YOU GAVE US LITTER, IN THE FORM OF GROUND UP SPENT BRIQUETTES!

WE MIXED YOU INTO THE MUDDY GROUND TO MAKE A SOLID GARDEN!

WHEN YOU THINK ABOUT IT, THIS CHARCOAL STOVE, SO INDISPENSABLE TO MOUNTAIN LIFE, IS OUR FRIEND...

FOR SIX MONTHS, YOU'VE MADE US HAPPY. YOU'VE MADE US REALLY AND TRULY HAPPY!

SEE YOU NEXT WINTER!

384

THE ROYALTIES CAME IN! ₩5,000,000—!!

HUG !

LET'S BUY A CAR!

LET'S PAY OUR OVERDUE INSURANCE AND TAX BILLS!

WE ALSO HAVE TO PAY BACK THE MONEY WE BORROWED FROM YOUR PROFESSOR.

...OF COURSE.

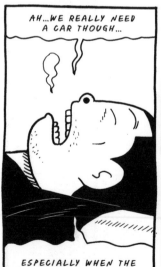

AH...WE REALLY NEED A CAR THOUGH...

ESPECIALLY WHEN THE SCHOOL YEAR BEGINS.

WHEN YOU GO TO THE CITY, I COULD DRIVE YOU THERE AND STUFF. WOULDN'T THAT BE GREAT?

PAY OFF OUR DEBTS FIRST!

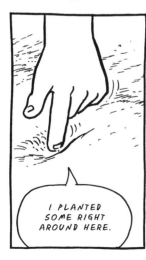

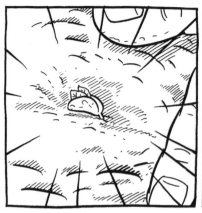

AH I EXPOSED IT!!

SORRY, SORRY!

FSSSHHHH —

FSSSSSHHHHHHH

GROW BIG AND STRONG.

YOU HAVE TO THIN THE SEEDLINGS SO THEY GROW BETTER.

OKAY.

THIS ONE'S LETTUCE!

THIS ONE'S SESAME!

THIS ONE'S MUGWORT!

STIR STIR

YOU MIX IN SESAME OIL AND RED PEPPER PASTE.

SPROUT BIBIMBAP FOR BREAKFAST!

CHOMP

SPROUT BIBIMBAP FOR LUNCH!

NOM

SPROUT BIBIMBAP FOR DINNER TOO??

IF WE THIN THE GARDEN EVERY DAY, THE SPROUTS WILL KEEP COMING, AND WE GOTTA KEEP EATING!

MY WIFE AND I WATERED AND WEEDED EVERY DAY, MORNING AND EVENING.

I'M KIND OF GROSSED OUT BY HOW ENDLESSLY THEY KEEP COMING UP.

HONEY, LOOK AT THIS.

HUH?

I DEFINITELY PULLED THIS WEED, ROOTS AND ALL, A FEW DAYS AGO, AND TOSSED IT ASIDE. LOOK AT IT NOW! IT JUST PUT DOWN MORE ROOTS AND EVEN GREW NEW LEAVES.

ISN'T THE LIFE FORCE OF WEEDS INCREDIBLE?

YOU GUYS MIGHT LIVE FIERCELY IN THE WILD...

BUT THERE'S NO ROOM FOR YOU IN THIS GARDEN.

LET'S GRILL MEAT FOR DINNER TONIGHT, HONEY! LIKE OLD TIMES.

WITH RICE WINE!

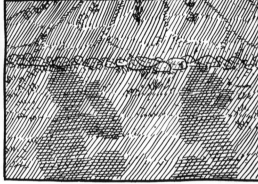

...HONEY, WHEN ARE THEY ANNOUNCING THE WINNERS OF THAT COMPETITION YOU ENTERED AGAIN?

GLUG GLUG GLUG

TOMORROW, OR MAYBE THE DAY AFTER?

IT'D BE GREAT IF YOU PLACED, BUT DON'T BE DISCOURAGED IF YOU DON'T.

GULP GULP

GETTING FEEDBACK ON YOUR WORK IS IMPORTANT TOO.

OF COURSE.

HONEY...

YES?

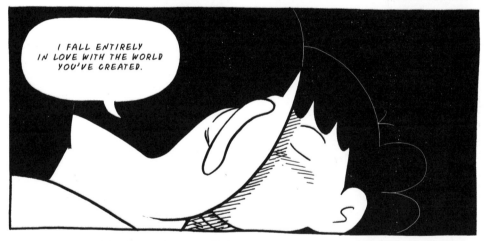

OH, NOW THAT I THINK ABOUT IT, THE PEPPER PLANTS HAVE GROWN TALL ENOUGH TO NEED STAKES IN THE GROUND.

I'LL GO CUT SOME WOOD UP ON THE MOUNTAIN AFTER LUNCH.

SIGH—THE DAY'S SO WARM, AND I REALLY WANT TO EAT BIBIM GUKSU.*

*THE NOODLE VERSION OF BIBIMBAP

YOU MAKE IT THIS TIME. I'LL STAND BY AND GUIDE YOU WHILE YOU MIX THE INGREDIENTS TOGETHER.

PFFF...

CLACK

394

ALL THE GARDENING WE'VE BEEN DOING THESE DAYS DOESN'T LEAVE MUCH TIME FOR WORK.

SLOUCH

GRRRUMBLE

STIR STIR

THANKS FOR LUNCH!

IS IT GOOD?

MM-HMM!

YOU DEFINITELY HAVE TO BE THE ONE TO MAKE THE BIBIM GUKSU FOR IT TO TASTE RIGHT.

SMACK SMACK

SLURRRP

YOU NEED TO TRY OR YOU WON'T GET BETTER. I MEAN, THE FACT THAT YOU STILL CAN'T TELL THE DIFFERENCE BETWEEN STORE-BOUGHT AND HOMEMADE SOY SAUCE...

WHEN I PUT MY MIND TO IT, I'M A GOOD COOK TOO.

HUH?

WHY ISN'T THAT BIRD FLAPPING ITS WINGS?

IT LOOKS LIKE IT'S HOVERING FOREVER IN THE WIND—

MIGHT BE A HAWK.

IT'S SO COOL!

A CUP OF COFFEE WOULD BE PERFECT RIGHT NOW.

I'D LIKE TO REQUEST A CUP FOR MYSELF AS WELL.

BRRRRIIIINNNG   BRRRRRIIIINNNG

WHILE YOU'RE UP GETTING THE PHONE, COFFEEEE!

ALL RIGHT ALREADY!

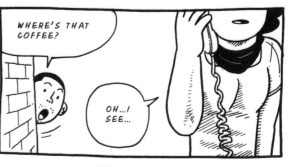

WHERE'S THAT COFFEE?

OH...I SEE...

...HONEY?

WOW—THAT'S REALLY AMAZING!!

I'M SO EXCITED!!

HOORAY HOORAY!

TODAY IS THE BEST!

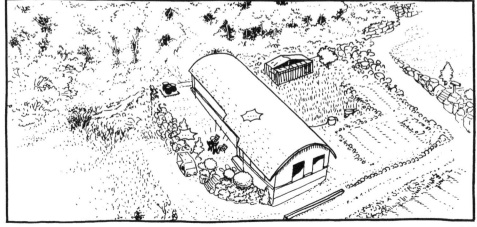

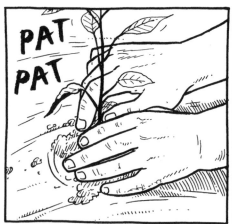

PAT
PAT

PLANTING
PEPPERS—

TOMATOES AND
EGGPLANTS
TOO...

WE'VE EVEN GOT
CUCUMBERS AND
SQUASH!

HONEY, I'M TURNING
THE WATER ON...

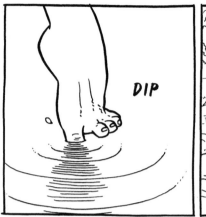

DIP

UGH, SO COLD!

YOU'RE BEING A BABY!

PTOO PTOO PTOO

SHRIEK!

MAY IS STILL COLD.

I'LL SAY.

THE NEXT DOOR NEIGHBOR IS HERE.

DRIP DRIP

DRIP

HE MUST BE COMING UP MORE OFTEN TO WEED HIS GARDEN.

MR. HONG! ISN'T IT STILL TOO EARLY TO BE SWIMMING?

HUH

YEAH, SEEMS LIKE IT!

HUH HUH

MY WIFE IS ABOUT TO
LEAVE FOR DENMARK.

FOR WINNING THE COMPETITION, SHE'S BEING PRESENTED WITH AWARD MONEY, AS WELL AS A FIVE-DAY TRIP TRAVELING AROUND HANS CHRISTIAN ANDERSEN'S HOMELAND.

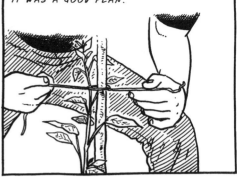

SHE ALSO WANTED TO TAKE THIS CHANCE TO GO TO FRANCE. I AGREED IT WAS A GOOD PLAN.

SO WHAT ARE YOU GOING TO DO BY YOURSELF FOR ELEVEN DAYS AND TEN NIGHTS?

WHAT DO YOU MEAN?

JUST GOING TO CLASS KEEPS ME BUSY.

ALSO, SINCE I NEED TO TEND TO THE GARDEN, I WON'T EVEN HAVE A SPARE MOMENT TO BE BORED.

THAT BEING SAID...

SINCE WE'VE BEEN TOGETHER— FOR OVER FOUR YEARS—WE'VE NEVER BEEN APART FOR LONGER THAN A WEEK.

SIGN: INCHEON AIRPORT LIMOUSINE BUS TERMINAL

SINCE WE DON'T HAVE MUCH WORK TO DO FOR ONCE, WANT TO COME OUT TO OUR PLACE?

YOU SAID YOUR WIFE IS IN EUROPE?

I WOULD BUT...WE'VE GOT CLASS TOMORROW, AND...

I DO WANT TO VISIT, BUT WHEN IT COMES RIGHT DOWN TO IT... POCHEON SEEMS REALLY FAR.

WELL, COME VISIT WHEN THE MOOD STRIKES YOU THEN. I'M GOING.

WANT TO GET A BEER INSTEAD?

NAH. I'VE GOT TO GET BACK AND DO SOME GARDENING.

SNIFF

SNIFF

WHY YOU LITTLE— WHY ARE YOU DIGGING RIGHT THERE?!

DIG

DIG

DIG

SHE MUST BE IN DENMARK BY NOW...

AFTER PREPARING AND REFINING FOR A LONG TIME, HER WORK HAS FINALLY COME TO FRUITION.

I'M AN ARTIST WHO DRAWS THOUGHTLESSLY, AND I TRIED TO TEACH MY WIFE THE SAME.

TEXT: LAIKA SPEAKS (DRAFT); PIGS WERE VERY SMART A LONG TIME AGO (DRAFT) BY SOHMI LEE   407

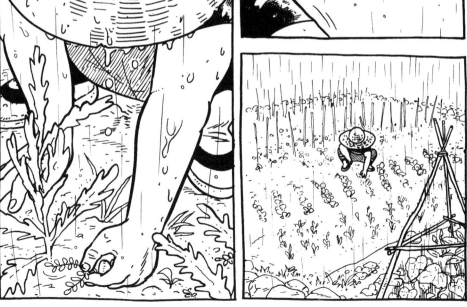

PULLING WEEDS IS MUCH EASIER BECAUSE OF THE RAIN.

THIS LAND, WHICH WAS OCCUPIED BY LITTER AND HIKER'S CARS...

IS NOW FULL OF THE LIFE WE SPREAD OVER IT.

HONEY, THIS IS YOUR MORNING CALL— WAKE UP!

IT'S EIGHT IN THE MORNING!

NNGGG...

I SAID IT'S 8:00 A.M., SO HURRY AND WAKE UP.

I'M AWAKE!

YOU'RE NOT SLEEPING?

RUMBLE

I'M AWAKE!

ALL RIGHT, HAVE SOME BREAKFAST.

THANK YOU.

NOW THAT THE GROUP ITINERARY IN DENMARK IS OVER AND SHE'S MOVED ON TO FRANCE ALONE, MY OVERSLEEPING WIFE HAS ASKED ME TO MAKE THESE MORNING CALLS.

413

THE FLOWERS HAVE DROPPED FROM THE STEMS, AND THESE CHERRY TOMATOES HAVE GROWN IN THEIR PLACE—

THE PEAS WEAVE BACK AND FORTH, AND STRETCH LIKE THEY'RE MEASURING THEIR OWN HEIGHT—

THE LETTUCE AND MUGWORT ARE ALREADY SO ABUNDANT... WILL YOU AND I BE ABLE TO EAT IT ALL?

416

PLUCK

HONEYYYYY—WHAT ABOUT THE MUGWORT?

I ALREADY GATHERED A BIT!

SEDUM

CRUNCH CRUNCH

NOM NOM

HOW WAS YOUR TRIP?

THERE WERE SO MANY CHARMING PLACES.

I WOULD HAVE BROUGHT YOU ALONG IF I'D HAD MORE MONEY.

PSH—EVEN IF WE HAD THE MONEY, I COULDN'T JUST PLAY HOOKY AND TRAVEL ALL OVER.

YEAH.

LET'S LOOK AT YOUR PHOTOS AFTER DINNER.

DID YOU HANG OUT WITH YOUR FRIENDS WHILE I WAS GONE?

LIKE I HAD THE TIME. I WAS VERY BUSY.

BUT YOU SAID YOU WERE BORED WITHOUT ME!

NOPE!

PFF

REALLY?

NOT AT ALL!!

PFFF

SIGN: AWARDS CEREMONY

2006

CHR

HONEY.

HONK HONK HONK

HONK

HOOONK

I WAS THINKING OF GETTING YOU A GIFT...

...WITH YOUR AWARD MONEY?

YEAH!

OOOH...THEN SHOULD I PICK OUT A COOL PAIR OF SNEAKERS?

C'MON, YOU KNOW!

THIS IS THE CAR. YA LIKE IT?

AH. YES!

WHEN D'YOU SAY YOU GOT YER LICENSE?

IT'S BEEN NEARLY EIGHT YEARS.

I'LL JUST DRIVE ONE TIME 'ROUND THE BLOCK, SO WATCH CAREFULLY, AND THEN YOU DRIVE.

WHAT?!

FROM ANSAN ALL THE WAY TO POCHEON?

YOU CAN JUS' FOLLOW MY CAR, SO DON'T WORRY TOO MUCH.

LIKE THIS. YOU KNOW TO PRESS THE GAS REAL LIGHT, RIGHT? YOU DON'T NEED TO HIT THE BRAKE TOO HARD NEITHER.

OKAY...OKAY...

STARTING TODAY...

THERE'S GOING TO BE A BIG DIFFERENCE IN THE SPEED AND DISTANCE I CAN TRAVEL.

I'VE GAINED THE FREEDOM TO GO WHEREVER I WANT...

VRRR OOOOOOM

ANYTIME, ANYWHERE!

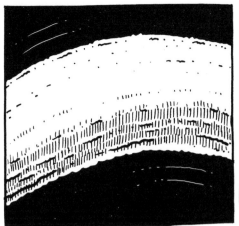

.....GOLDIE.....

.....GOLDIE.....

GOLDIE, DINNER TIME—

SILVIE—
OAKIE—

DINNER TIME—

THEY'RE COMING DOWN OVER THERE!

MEOWWW

THEY MUST HAVE BEEN ON THE OTHER SIDE OF THE MOUNTAIN!

THEY'RE EX- PANDING THEIR TERRITORY.

THOSE GUYS.

GIVE THEM SOME DINNER. I'LL WEED SOME MORE AND THEN COME INSIDE.

BUT WE WERE GOING TO GO TO KOMORI FOR DINNER!

OH, RIGHT!

I TOLD MY WIFE ABOUT ONE OF THE THINGS I WROTE WHILE SHE WAS AWAY.

THAT'S A GOOD IDEA. YOU SHOULD WRITE A SHORT STORY BASED ON IT.

HAHA, SHOULD I?

IT'S NICE TO SEE YOU LOOK SO HAPPY, HONEY.

WELL, SINCE THERE AREN'T ANY DEADLINES CHASING ME DOWN...

I WANT TO HELP YOU MORE SO YOU CAN SPEND TIME ON YOUR OWN PROJECTS.

JUST KEEP DOING WHAT YOU'RE DOING. I STILL HAVE TO COMPLETE THE MANU-SCRIPT AND TAKE IT TO A PUBLISHER!

OKAY.

AHHH! THAT DINNER WAS GREAT.

I MIGHT TAKE A LOOK AT THE GARDEN.

OH MY—THESE CUCUMBERS LOOK REALLY ENTICING.

SHUT

I CAN EAT ONE, RIGHT?

!

NO. DON'T PICK IT.

HAHAHA... WELLL...

WE'VE ONLY PLANTED A FEW CUCUMBERS, JUST ENOUGH FOR OURSELVES.

W-WE TEND A BIGGER GARDEN THAN THIS.

THEN YOU CAN GO HOME AND PICK WHAT YOU WANT.

IT'S A GOOD THING I HAD MY MIND SWITCH TURNED OFF...

IF I WERE MYSELF, I'D HAVE JUST, BOOM—!!

CRACK

I MEAN, AFTER ALL THAT WORK, IF EACH HIKER TOOK A CUCUMBER, WHAT WOULD BE LEFT?

THANKS, BRO.

GOOD OL' COUNTRY HOSPITALITY!

CRUNCH CRUNCH

I DON'T EVEN KNOW WHAT WOULD HAVE HAPPENED IF HE HAD ACTUALLY PICKED THAT CUCUMBER.

WHAT'S A MIND SWITCH?

IT'S A KIND OF MIND CONTROL, OF COURSE.

I LEARNED IT FROM YOU.

WHAT? I DIDN'T TEACH YOU THAT!

HERE'S AN
ILLUSTRATION:
IN MY MIND THERE
ARE A VARIETY OF
EMOTIONS I CAN
TURN ON OR OFF
WITH A SWITCH.
FOR EXAMPLE,
ANGER, SADNESS,
SHAME, FEAR...

ANGER

SADNESS

AS LONG AS
THESE EMOTIONS
CAN BE STOPPED
BEFORE REACHING
CRITICAL LEVELS...

BUT HOW?

WHEN AN OCCASION FOR ANGER ARISES,
LIKE EARLIER, I CUT OFF THE POWER
SUPPLY FOR THAT EMOTION, MEANING
I IMAGINE TURNING OFF AN ACTUAL
"ANGER" SWITCH.

I CONJURE
THIS IMAGE IN
MY MIND:

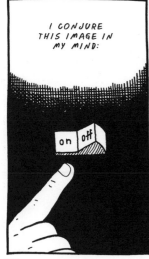

 CLICK

 CLICK

 CLICK

REMEMBER LATE LAST YEAR, WHEN I REACHED MY LIMIT, MENTALLY AND PHYSICALLY?

...YOU REALLY DID, HONEY.

CRAAAWL...

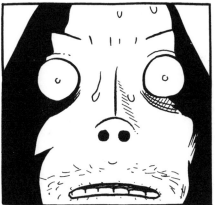

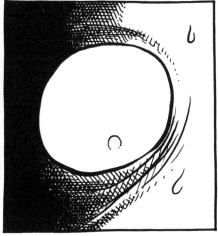

WHEN MY PESSIMISM ABOUT MYSELF AND THE WORLD WAS CONSTANT, SOMETHING HAPPENED...

IS IT AN ANT?

HUH? WHERE'D IT GO?

YOU AWAKE?

· · ·

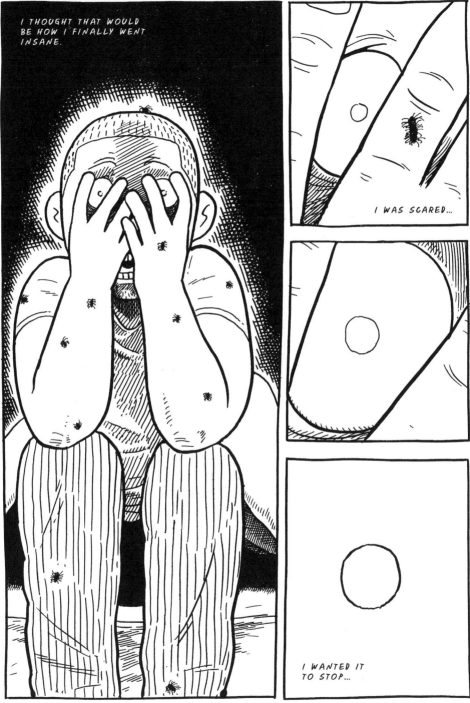

433

WHAT'S ON YOUR MIND?

AH!

. . .

THE MOMENT I REALIZED THE LIMITATIONS OF MY BODY AND MY MIND, EVERYTHING RESET FROM THE PAIN, LIKE A FILAMENT SNAPPING IN HALF.

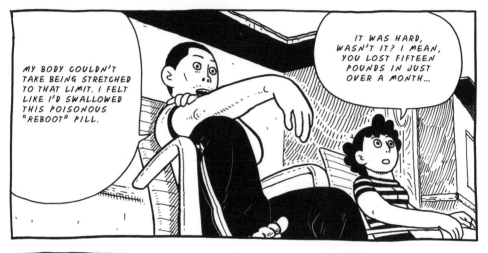

MY BODY COULDN'T TAKE BEING STRETCHED TO THAT LIMIT. I FELT LIKE I'D SWALLOWED THIS POISONOUS "REBOOT" PILL.

IT WAS HARD, WASN'T IT? I MEAN, YOU LOST FIFTEEN POUNDS IN JUST OVER A MONTH...

IT WAS AWFUL, CONTINUALLY MAKING MYSELF SICK, THEN HAVING TO TAKE MEDICINE OVER AND OVER AGAIN...

SO I BUILT THIS MIND SWITCH INTO MY BRAIN.

IT'S A GOOD TACTIC, BUT I DON'T REMEMBER TEACHING IT TO YOU.

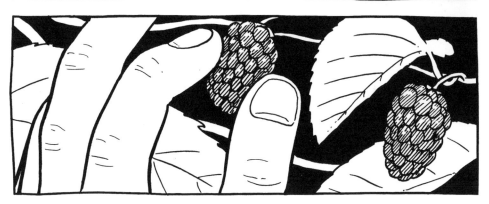

435

OW—MY NECK... MY ARM'S ASLEEP TOO. I CAN'T PICK ANYMORE.

KEEP PICKING. IT'S NOT ENOUGH TO MAKE EXTRACT YET!

OH, AND I WAS SEARCHING ON THE INTERNET, AND IT SAID WILD PEACHES NEED TO BE PICKED BEFORE THE SEED HARDENS.

YOU MEAN THAT TREE NEAR THE VALLEY YOU TOLD ME ABOUT?

LET'S PICK THOSE PEACHES TOMORROW; THERE'S ALSO A PATCH OF LIGULARIA NEAR THE VALLEY THAT I WANTED TO PICK.

YOU CAN IDENTIFY LIGULARIA?!

I MEAN, IT'S AN HERB I REALLY LIKE, SO I KNEW IT WHEN I SAW IT.

IMPRESSIVE.

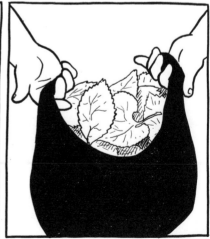

WHAT DID YOU SAY?!

DANG IT—I WANTED TO PICK SOME MORE...

COMING—!

WE SHOULD GET OFF THE MOUNTAIN BEFORE SUNSET.

I PICKED A BUNCH OF MUL-BERRIES!

OAKIE! LET'S GO!

WOW, YOU PICKED A LOT!

IT'S RAIN!

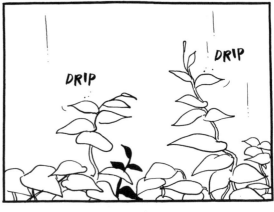

DRIP

DRIP

LET'S MOVE IT ALONG!

SLOW DOWN, THE RAIN'S NICE AND COOL!

FOOSH

BUT IT'S REALLY COMIN' DOWN!

GOTCHA!

SLOW DOWN!

WHEN IT SNOWS, YOU WANT TO FREEZE; WHEN IT RAINS, YOU WANT TO GET WET. YOU'RE CRAZY!

THIS FEELS GREAT!!

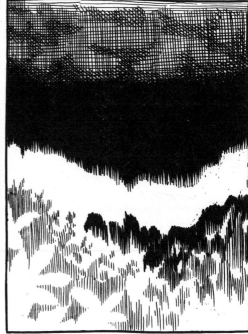

WOO HOO! IT'S GYERAN MARI!*

I'M NOT SURE HOW IT TASTES.

...SHOULD WE RAISE CHICKENS TOO, AND EAT THE EGGS?

CATS, A DOG, AND NOW CHICKENS?

*A ROLLED OMELETTE

GOOD TO SEE THE SUN OUT AGAIN!

HURRY AND STAKE THE BROKEN BEAN STALKS.

HOLD ON! LISTEN CAREFULLY.

?

LATELY, I'VE BEEN HEARING THIS SOUND ALL DAY.

BRR...

RRRRUMBLE

GRUMBLE

IS IT THUNDER RUMBLING FROM REALLY FAR AWAY? BUT THE SKY IS CLEAR...

444

COUNTLESS STREAMS FROM NUMEROUS MOUNTAINS GATHER IN WANGSUKCHEON RIVER AND FORM A COLOSSAL MONSTER THAT SLIDES ALONG.

LET'S GO BACK HOME. I'M AFRAID OF THE WATER NOW.

BUT YOU WERE THE ONE WHO WANTED TO COME DOWN HERE TO HAVE A LOOK!

WE LIVED THROUGH MULTIPLE BLACKOUTS AND PHONE OUTAGES, AND THEN THE MONSOONS PASSED, JUST LIKE THAT.

Summer

SPLASH

I'M UNDERWATER TOO—

AH, MY BODY KEEPS FLOATING.

GRAB MY HANDS.

OKAY.

I'M SINKING TO THE BOTTOM.

ME TOO.

449

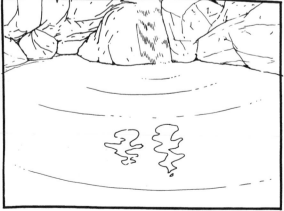

THE— SKY—

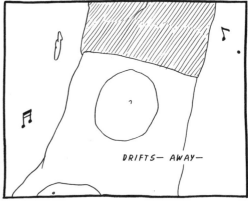

DRIFTS— AWAY—

AND— THE— CLOUDS— DRIFT— AWAY—

THERE— IS— NOTHING—
TO— HOLD— US— DOWN—

MY— WIFE— AND— I—
BOTH— DRIFT— AWAY—

YOU DRAW FAST...

AND THAT'S FINE, BUT I WISH YOU'D DRAW WITH MORE SINCERITY.

THAT'S JUST MY STYLE. YOU KNOW, WHEN YOU WORK, YOU FRET TOO LONG OVER EACH DRAWING!

WHO, ME?

LIKE THE PROJECT YOU'RE WORKING ON NOW. YOU CRITIQUE ME, BUT WHAT HAVE YOU DONE IN THIS THREE-MONTH GAP?

OH... WELL...

WHEN I'M WORKING, I JUST GET IT DONE. I CAN'T WORK INSIDE MY OWN HEAD LIKE YOU.

YEAH, BUT THE QUALITY OF YOUR DRAWING IS JUST...

I'M COMPLETELY FINE WITH THE QUALITY, SO I DON'T KNOW WHY YOU KEEP BRINGING IT UP...

FINE THEN.

WAS I TOO HARSH?

SORRY, HONEY.

JUST LEAVE THAT DUDE ALONE. LET'S GO TO TOEGYEWON TO BUY SOME CHICKENS.

HE'S IN THE MIDDLE OF WONDERING WHAT HE'S BEEN DOING FOR THREE MONTHS.

THAT'S A RELIEF.

IT'S BEEN NEARLY A YEAR SINCE Y'ALL MOVED HERE, RIGHT?

YES, IT'S BEEN ABOUT TEN MONTHS.

AFTER BEING SICK ALL WINTER, I FINALLY THINK I'LL SURVIVE.

HO HO HO, THAT'S NATURAL. WHEN YOU MOVE TO THIS KIND OF ENVIRONMENT, YOU HAVE TO SHED THE GRIME OF THE CITY TO ADAPT.

YOU'LL BE FINE.

SINCE WE CAN'T COME OUT HERE THAT OFTEN, WOULD YOU WATER OUR LAWN, WHENEVER YOU HAPPEN TO THINK OF IT?

OF COURSE, DON'T WORRY ABOUT IT.

PEPPERS, LETTUCE— JUST HELP YOURSELVES TO OUR GARDEN.

OH, THANK YOU SO MUCH.

CHEEP
CHEEP
CHIRP
CHIRP
TWEET

NOW IT'S BACK TO JUST THE TWO OF US AGAIN.

UH-HUH.

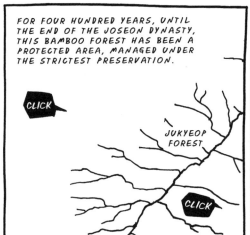

FOR FOUR HUNDRED YEARS, UNTIL THE END OF THE JOSEON DYNASTY, THIS BAMBOO FOREST HAS BEEN A PROTECTED AREA, MANAGED UNDER THE STRICTEST PRESERVATION.

CLICK

JUKYEOP FOREST

CLICK

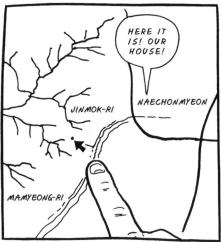

HERE IT IS! OUR HOUSE!

JINMOK-RI

NAECHONMYEON

MAMYEONG-RI

WHAT A CHARMING PLACE.

WHAT IS?

THIS MOUNTAIN WE LIVE ON. IT'S FILLED WITH ANCIENT CONIFERS. IT MAY NOT OFFICIALLY BE AN ARBORETUM, BUT WHEN YOU SEE THE WAY THEY'VE TIRELESSLY PRESERVED THE TREES...

459

ASIDE FROM LOCAL VIL-
LAGERS ON WALKS, THERE
REALLY NEEDS TO BE SOME
SORT OF REGULATION ON
OUTSIDERS ENTERING
THE MOUNTAIN.

IF YOU REALLY THINK
ABOUT IT, WE'RE
OUTSIDERS TOO.

WHAT ARE WE,
TRAMPS?

WE PUT IN OUR
TRANSFER REPORT, SO
WE ARE OFFICIALLY
CITIZENS OF THIS
VILLAGE. IN FACT,
WE'RE CITIZENS OF
THIS MOUNTAIN.

BUT HONEY...

HM?

I'M SET TO FINISH
MY MANUSCRIPT
TODAY, SO LET'S
MAKE SOME TIME
AND GO TALK TO
PAJU PUBLISHING.

Y-YOU'RE ALREADY
DONE?!

THUD

GETTING A FEW BUCKS AND AN AWARD IS ONE THING, BUT GETTING PUBLISHED IS SOMETHING ELSE.

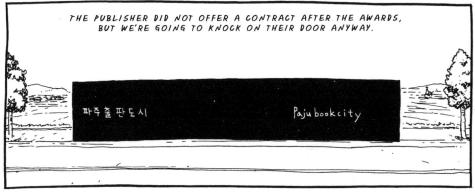

THE PUBLISHER DID NOT OFFER A CONTRACT AFTER THE AWARDS, BUT WE'RE GOING TO KNOCK ON THEIR DOOR ANYWAY.

파주출판도시

Pajubookcity

THE APPRAISAL WILL BE DISPASSIONATE.

I'M ANXIOUS ABOUT A FEW PAGES.

...I'M WORRIED.

SO ENTERTAINING AND UNIQUE!

WE'D LIKE TO MAKE A DEAL WITH YOU IMMEDIATELY FOR BOTH OF THESE STORIES, SOHMI LEE!

THE DRAWINGS ARE SO FUN.

I LIKE THE SUBJECT. AND IT'S WELL DRAWN.

RIGHT? LOOK AT THE COLOR RIGHT HERE.

465

ONCE THE PARTIAL REVISIONS
ARE COMPLETED, THE FIRST BOOK
IS EXPECTED TO BE RELEASED BY
THE END OF THE YEAR.

THE PUBLISHERS SAW MY WIFE'S WORK WITH A DIFFERENT EYE THAN MINE. WHERE I SAW MISTAKES, THEY SAW TRACES OF ORIGINALITY.

FRANKLY, I WAS BEWILDERED.

I TRIED TO TEACH MY WIFE TO DRAW THE WAY I WAS TAUGHT, BUT IN THE END, MY ADVICE COULD HAVE BEEN TOXIC...

IT'S LIKE I TOOK A CHILD WHO WANTED NOTHING MORE THAN TO DRAW ON PAPER, AND PLOPPED A HOW-TO-DRAW BOOK IN FRONT OF HER INSTEAD.

HERE I COME!

VROOM...

VRM... VROOM...

PULL FORWARD S'MORE!

GO DOWN TO THE VALLEY AND GRAB US A SPOT!

PROPANE TANKS AND DOG MEAT. EVEN A BOX OF LIQUOR...

NOISY SINGING...

469

THESE PEOPLE HAVE NO RESPECT. THIS IS A RESTRICTED AREA.

I KNOW IT'S A HOLIDAY...BUT I DIDN'T THINK THAT THERE WOULD BE THIS MANY CARS...

WELL, THERE ARE ALWAYS GOING TO BE TOURISTS WHO DON'T UNDERSTAND THE DIFFERENCE BETWEEN THE CITY AND THE COUNTRY.

THEY CAN PUT UP A "NO ENTRY" SIGN ALL THEY WANT, BUT IT WON'T MAKE A LICK OF DIFFERENCE.

NO MATTER HOW MANY CARS SWARM THE MOUNTAIN, NO MATTER HOW MUCH DOG MEAT THEY GRILL ON THEIR PROPANE STOVES, AND NO MATTER HOW MUCH TRASH THEY LEAVE BEHIND, THESE ARE MOSTLY PEOPLE FROM OUR OWN NEIGHBORHOOD.

PURR PURR PURR

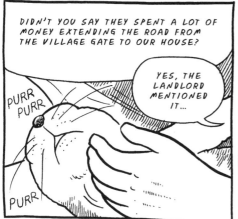

DIDN'T YOU SAY THEY SPENT A LOT OF MONEY EXTENDING THE ROAD FROM THE VILLAGE GATE TO OUR HOUSE?

YES, THE LANDLORD MENTIONED IT...

PURR PURR

PURR

BASICALLY, THE VILLAGE COMPENSATED THEM AND CLEANED UP THE STREET, AND NOW THE VILLAGERS BRING THEIR CARS AND USE IT AS A PARKING LOT.

IF THE VILLAGERS ARE GOING TO BE LIKE THIS, THE OWNER SHOULDN'T HAVE BOTHERED IN THE FIRST PLACE.

...

I WANT TO BELIEVE THAT MOST PEOPLE MEAN WELL, BUT ALL I SEE HERE IS GREED.

THE VILLAGE'S WATER SUPPLY STARTS RIGHT ABOVE SEONNYEO POOL*, AND YET THE VILLAGE ADMINISTRATOR HAS NEVER BEEN UP THERE?

SOME- THING REEKS...

I TOOK THOSE LITTER PHOTOS AND PUT THEM RIGHT UNDER HIS NOSE. HE TOSSED OUT SOME EMPTY PROMISES, AND HERE WE ARE A FEW DAYS LATER WITH NO NEWS.

IF THINGS KEEP GOING LIKE THIS...

WHAT, YOU'LL DE- VISE ANOTHER SCHEME?

*SEONNYEOTANG, OR FAIRY BATH, IS THE FABLED SITE OF THE HEAVENLY MAIDEN AND THE WOODCUTTER FOLKTALE

TEXT: YESTERDAY'S TRASH

IS IT REALLY NECESSARY TO GO TO SUCH LENGTHS?

I'M PLANNING TO STOP NOW.

SCRITCH SCRATCH

EVEN I DON'T HAVE THE ENERGY TO KEEP DOING THIS.

WHEW~

I HAVE TO TURN THE SOIL SO WE CAN PLANT FALL CABBAGE AND DAIKON.

OOF

OVER THE MONTH OF AUGUST, WE HAD PLENTY OF VISITORS TO OUR HOME TOO.

MY WIFE'S STUDY GROUP RETREAT

MY SISTER-IN-LAW'S FAMILY VACATION

YEONGJI MUSHROOMS!

OLD COLLEGE BUDDY HANGOUT

AND SOME OF MY YOUNGER COLLEGE FRIENDS TOO...

THERE'S SOME TRASH OVER THERE!

OKAY!

WE HAD SO MUCH FUN!

WE'LL VISIT AGAIN SOON!

VROOM...

내촌 청림

11

VRM...

WHEW—I'M BEAT...

DID YOU SEND THEM OFF?

UH-HUH!

THE CHICKEN FEED IS RUNNING LOW.

WELL, THEY'RE ALSO EATING PLANTS AND WORMS AND BUGS, SO WE CAN GIVE THEM MORE FEED TOMORROW.

SHOULD WE, THOUGH?

479

YES, WELL...TO LEAVE IT SEEMED LIKE A WASTE.

I HAVEN'T BEEN HERE SINCE I WAS A CHILD...I USED TO VISIT THIS VALLEY.

LOCAL JOURNALIST...!

THESE DAYS, MANY PEOPLE COME UP THE MOUNTAIN. IT WOULD BE FINE IF THEY DIDN'T LITTER, BUT THEY TOSS THEIR TRASH SO CARELESSLY.

IS THAT SO?

THE TRUTH IS, THIS ENTIRE AREA USED TO BE A CHESTNUT TREE FOREST.

AT LEAST BEFORE ANY HOUSES WERE BUILT.

THAT AREA OVER THERE, WHERE THE BRIDGE STANDS, USED TO BE AN EXPANSIVE VALLEY, BUT OUTSIDERS BOUGHT THE LAND AND FILLED IT UP.

DID YOU KNOW THAT?

MY RING MUST HAVE FALLEN INTO THE WATER WHEN WE WERE SWIMMING.

IT'S TOO LATE NOW, SO I'LL LOOK FOR IT TOMORROW.

WOOSH

WHOOOO—

SCRITCH
SCRATCH

THAT'S THE SECOND RING I'VE LOST. IF I CAN'T FIND IT, MY WIFE WILL BE VERY UPSET. SHE HAD TO MELT DOWN HER OWN NECKLACE TO MAKE IT.

ZZZ ZZZ

WHOOOO

WHOOOOOSH

IF THE FRONT YARD WAS JUST A GRAVEL OR DIRT LOT, WE WOULDN'T HAVE TO GO TO THE TROUBLE OF PULLING WEEDS...

IF YOU WANT A NICE LAWN TO LOOK AT, KEEP PICKIN'!

THESE DAMN PLANTAGO WEEDS ARE JUST AS TOUGH AS THEIR NAME SUGGESTS.* THE LEAVES MIGHT BE SMALL, BUT THE ROOTS GO DEEP.

THWACK THWACK

UGH, MY BACK!

LET'S GO TO SEONNYEO POOL!!

...AFTER WE FEED THE CHICKENS.

482 *THE KOREAN WORD FOR PLANTAGO (질경이) SOUNDS SIMILAR TO THE WORD FOR TOUGH OR TENACIOUS (질겨)

I LOOKED IT UP, AND THESE LINDEN TREE SEEDS CAN BE DISTILLED INTO ESSENTIAL OIL, AND THE LEAVES CAN BE BOILED TO MAKE TEA.

LOOKS RIPE

IS IT TRUE THAT BUDDHA REACHED NIRVANA UNDERNEATH A LINDEN TREE?

UGHHH SO SOUR!

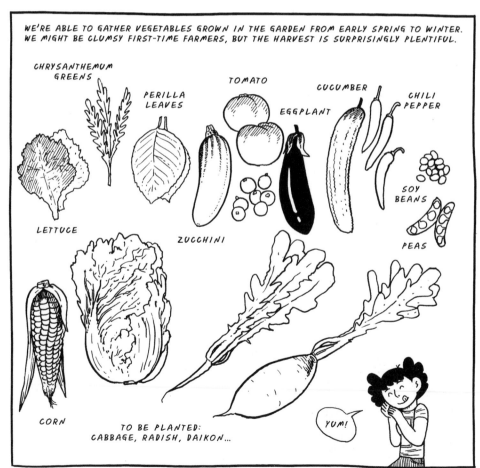

WE'RE ABLE TO GATHER VEGETABLES GROWN IN THE GARDEN FROM EARLY SPRING TO WINTER. WE MIGHT BE CLUMSY FIRST-TIME FARMERS, BUT THE HARVEST IS SURPRISINGLY PLENTIFUL.

CHRYSANTHEMUM GREENS

PERILLA LEAVES

TOMATO

CUCUMBER

EGGPLANT

CHILI PEPPER

LETTUCE

ZUCCHINI

SOY BEANS

PEAS

CORN

TO BE PLANTED: CABBAGE, RADISH, DAIKON...

YUM!

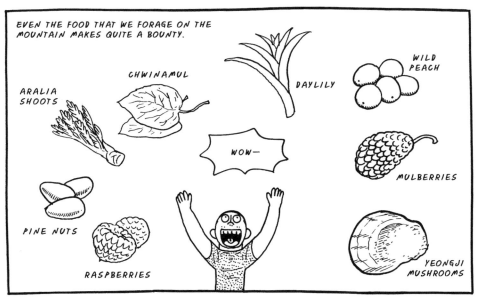

EVEN THE FOOD THAT WE FORAGE ON THE MOUNTAIN MAKES QUITE A BOUNTY.

CHWINAMUL

DAYLILY

WILD PEACH

ARALIA SHOOTS

WOW—

MULBERRIES

PINE NUTS

RASPBERRIES

YEONGJI MUSHROOMS

OF COURSE, THERE MUST BE DOZENS OF VARIETIES OF WILD EDIBLE PLANTS ON THE MOUNTAIN THAT WE DON'T KNOW ABOUT, BUT WE JUST AREN'T SURE.

...LAST SPRING, I REMEMBER SEEING SOME OLD WOMEN COMING DOWN FROM THE MOUNTAIN, EACH HAULING A FULL BURLAP SACK.

IS THERE ANY WAY TO DIG UP MORE VARIETIES OF SPRING PLANTS NEXT YEAR?

OUTSIDE OF FOL-LOWING AROUND THE OLD LADIES FROM THE VILLAGE?

ONCE THE HENS LAY EGGS AND PROVIDE ANIMAL PROTEIN, WE'LL BE SELF-SUFFICIENT! THAT'S QUITE A HEALTHY DIET.

BULGE

SHOULD WE RAISE PIGS TOO?!

485

WE FOUND AN ABANDONED TRAP IN STORAGE, AND I SET IT OUT TO CATCH FISH.

HERE.

AH!

BRRRRRING
BEEP

HELLO?

CHANG-CHANG, IT'S ME.

SO TASTY.

YOU DIDN'T EVEN VISIT DURING THE HOLIDAY SEASON, SO COME ON OUT NOW.

RIGHT NOW?!

BUT POCHEON IS TOO FAR—

WHAT DO YOU MEAN, "FAR"? IT'S AN HOUR FROM CHEONG-NYANGNI.

I CAN PICK YOU UP IN TOWN.

I HAVE SOME WORK TO DO...

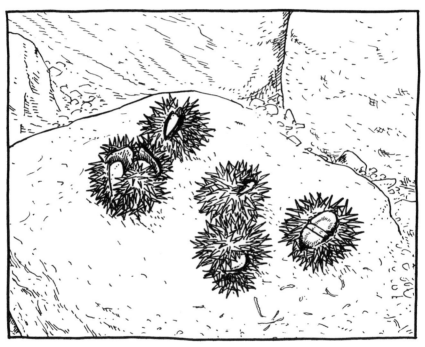

Fall

CLACK

HAVE A TASTE. IT'S LINDEN TEA.

MY GOODNESS, DID YOU PREPARE THIS FROM SCRATCH?

OH HO, IT'S DELICIOUS.

...SO, DO YOU ENJOY DAILY LIFE HERE?

THE SCENT IS LOVELY...

YES, I'VE TOTALLY LOST MYSELF IN THE JOY OF RAISING A VEGETABLE GARDEN.

WE WERE SO SURPRISED WHEN WE SAW THE BACK LOT HAD BEEN TRANSFORMED INTO A GARDEN.

I THOUGHT YOU MUST BOTH BE LIVING SUCH A BEAUTIFUL LIFE...

AND DID YOU SAY YOU HEAT THE HOUSE WITH COAL IN THE WINTER?

THANKS TO THAT, WE'VE SAVED ON ENERGY COSTS, AND WE STILL ENJOY A WARM HOME.

MY HUSBAND WANTED TO VISIT THE NEIGHBORHOOD GOLF COURSE, SO WE THOUGHT WE'D STOP BY HERE ON THE WAY BACK. WE GAVE YOU NO NOTICE, SO YOU MUST HAVE BEEN SURPRISED TO SEE US!

OH NO, NOT AT ALL...

WE HAD BEEN WONDERING IF YOU MIGHT EVER VISIT THE HOUSE.

WE'VE ALSO RAISED DOGS HERE, RAISED CHICKENS, HAVE GROWN A GARDEN, AND FOUND OUR HEALTH, BUT THESE DAYS, DAILY LIFE IN SEOUL CONSTANTLY CHASES US DOWN. WE'RE SO BUSY.

HERE...WE GREW THESE IN THE GARDEN.

OH, YOU DIDN'T HAVE TO GO TO THE TROUBLE...

IT'S GREAT TO SEE BOTH OF YOU GROWING VEGETABLES AND LIVING SO WELL.

MY MOM ALSO LIVED HERE WITH US FOR MANY YEARS, BUT SHE'S MOVED BACK TO SEOUL TOO...

SHE THINKS ABOUT THE OLD NEIGHBORHOOD A LOT. SHE KEEPS SAYING SHE WANTS TO COME BACK, TO LIVE HERE AGAIN.

OH... REALLY...?

BUT SHE NEEDS TO STAY IN SEOUL, SO SHE CAN VISIT THE HOSPITAL AND GO TO MASS REGULARLY.

SLAM

...

WAG WAG

. . .

PANT PANT PANT

PANT

PANT PANT

TOK TOK
TOK
TOK
TOK

SHAKE IT HARDER!

VRM...

SOUNDS LIKE THEY'RE PLANNING TO DO SOME LANDSCAPE CONSTRUCTION AROUND THE HOUSE.

WHAT?

HOW CAN THEY DO CONSTRUCTION WHILE WE'RE LIVING HERE?!

I ASKED THEM TO POSTPONE IT, BUT THERE ARE SO MANY SUNKEN AREAS THAT THEY NEED TO HURRY...

HOW CAN THEY DO THIS? HOW ARE WE SUPPOSED TO WORK?!

THEY SAY IT WILL TAKE A WEEK AT MOST. THERE'S NOTHING WE CAN DO ABOUT IT.

OH, AND THEY ASKED ABOUT INSTALLING AN ENERGY EFFICIENT ELECTRIC BOILER TOO.

SINCE THEY'RE ASKING ABOUT THE BOILER ON TOP OF ALL THIS LANDSCAPING, IT SEEMS LIKE THEY'VE BEEN PLANNING ALL THIS FOR A WHILE. THEY'LL PROBABLY EITHER SELL THE HOUSE OR MOVE BACK.

501

WHEN WE FIRST MOVED HERE, WE SIGNED THE LEASE BECAUSE THEY SAID WE COULD LIVE HERE FOR AS LONG AS WE WANTED...

WELL, LET'S NOT JUMP TO CONCLUSIONS YET. IF THEY INSTALL AN ELECTRIC BOILER, AT LEAST WE'LL GET TO ENJOY IT.

OH NO!

IF THEY'RE LANDSCAPING, WHAT'S GOING TO HAPPEN TO OUR GARDEN? ARE THEY GETTING RID OF IT?

...YEAH.

THEY'RE HAULING IN MORE DIRT TO LEVEL AND RAISE THE SURFACE... I GUESS IT'LL BE EASIER TO PLANT ANOTHER GARDEN...

ALL THAT WORK WE PUT INTO THE GARDEN WAS FOR NOTHING...

MEOW

HONEY...?

...YOU ASLEEP?

NO.

· · ·

...WHY?

SHOULD WE...
BUY SOME
LAND?

HM? WHAT ARE
YOU TALKING
ABOUT?

THE TRUTH IS,
EARLIER IN THE DAY,
THE OWNER...

IF WE DO END UP
MOVING BACK INTO THE
HOUSE, THERE'S A WAY
FOR YOU AND YOUR
WIFE TO CONTINUE
LIVING HERE.

YOU'D BE ABLE TO TAKE OUT A LOAN AGAINST
OUR CREDIT. WHAT WOULD YOU THINK ABOUT
BUILDING A PREFABRICATED HOUSE ON PART
OF THE LOT AND LIVING THERE?

SHE SAID THEY CAN ERECT A PREFAB HOUSE PRETTY QUICKLY THESE DAYS, AND SINCE IT'S ON THE CHEAP SIDE, IF WE GOT A LOAN...

...SO WE BUILD MORE DEBT AS WE BUILD A HOUSE...?

ARGH! IF ONLY WE OWNED SOME LAND IN THE NEIGHBORHOOD...

HONEY, IT'S NOT LAND THAT WE NEED, BUT A HOUSE TO LIVE IN.

WHAT IF...WHAT IF WE HAVE TO LEAVE HERE SOONER THAN WE PLANNED?

I WANT TO KEEP LIVING HERE...

. . . .

ZZZ...
ZZZ...

OUR GARDEN HAS DISAPPEARED.

WE REMOVED ROCKS, PLUCKED THE PEBBLES, AND PUT OUR HANDS IN THE DIRT TENDERLY, LIKE TO A BABY'S SKIN. EVERY RIDGE AND FURROW OF THIS FIELD, ALL TRACES OF IT HAVE VANISHED BEFORE OUR EYES.

UGH, SO NOISY.

IN THE DAYTIME, DURING CONSTRUCTION, WE HAD TO LEAVE THE HOUSE TO ESCAPE THE NOISE.

WE SPENT NEARLY TEN DAYS LIKE THIS.

HOW'S THE SCRIPT GOING?

SO-SO.

SIGN: FISHING AND SWIMMING PROHIBITED

IT'S FALL AGAIN...

MM-HM.

...I'VE SEEN THAT MAN BEFORE. HE MUST BE THE OWNER OF THE LAND BACK BY THE VALLEY. HIS FACE IS ALWAYS TWISTED, EXPRESSING JUDGMENT.

GLIMPSE

SLAM

VROOM

WHAT THE HELL? HE PRETENDED HE DIDN'T SEE ME, JUST LIKE LAST TIME.

I'VE GOT A BAD FEELING ABOUT HIM...

I HAVE AFTER-NOON CLASS, SO I'M GOING OUT TO SEOUL.

REALLY?!

NOM NOM

WE'RE OUT OF DRAWING PAPER. CAN YOU PICK SOME UP ON YOUR WAY BACK?

SURE.

ONCE THEY INSTALL THE BOILER, I GUESS WE WON'T NEED TO STOKE THE CHARCOAL BRIQUETTES ANYMORE.

WHY NOT?

WHAT DO YOU MEAN? WE'LL HAVE THE CHEAP AND EASY ELECTRIC BOILER. WHAT'LL WE NEED CHARCOAL FOR?

THE CHARCOAL STOVE IS PRETTY ELEGANT, AND WE CAN BOIL WATER ON IT...

HM.

FROM THE POSITION OF THE GUY WHO HAS TO CHANGE THE SPENT CHARCOAL BRIQUETTES, I'M INCLINED TO DISAGREE.

IF YOU REALLY WANT TO USE IT, I CAN INSTALL IT FOR YOU, BUT ONLY IF YOU CHANGE THE SPENT BRIQUETTES.

WHAT'S WITH THE ATTITUDE?

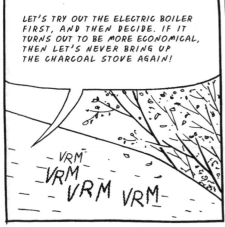

LET'S TRY OUT THE ELECTRIC BOILER FIRST, AND THEN DECIDE. IF IT TURNS OUT TO BE MORE ECONOMICAL, THEN LET'S NEVER BRING UP THE CHARCOAL STOVE AGAIN!

VRM
VRM
VRM VRM

A FEW DAYS LATER, THE ELECTRIC BOILER REPLACED THE OIL BOILER.

VRM
VRM

VRM
VRM VRM

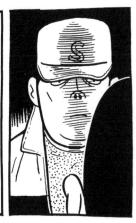

THIS BIG ROOM IS ALWAYS STUFFY. WHAT IF WE PUT IN A LARGE GLASS DOOR?

WELL, IT WON'T BE HUMID DURING CONSTRUCTION.

...CONSTRUCTION?

AH...

FOR SOME REASON, MY MOTHER INSISTS ON RETURNING HERE.

WE DON'T KNOW THE EXACT DATE YET, BUT WE'RE THINKING ABOUT BRINGING HER HERE NEXT SPRING.

BUT WE'RE STILL LIVING HERE. CAN'T YOU DELAY CONSTRUCTION UNTIL AFTER WE'VE MOVED OUT?

THE PROCESS WILL BE EXPEDITED. PLEASE GIVE US YOUR CONSENT ONE LAST TIME.

517

...LAST YEAR IT WAS SO COLD, WE SLEPT IN THE CORNER OF THE LIVING ROOM BY THE STOVE, BUT NOW WE'RE ACTUALLY SLEEPING IN THE BEDROOM.

THERE'S NOTHING WE CAN DO...

THE MOST WE COULD DO WAS ASK THEM TO DELAY CONSTRUCTION FOR A FEW DAYS...

WE AREN'T OWNERS— NOT OF THIS HOUSE, NOT OF THIS MOUNTAIN.

IF WE'RE SUPPOSED TO LEAVE IN A MONTH, WE HAVE TO FIND ANOTHER PLACE TO MOVE TO IMMEDIATELY. WE'RE MERE TENANTS. THAT'S OUR LOT.

LET'S...

M-O-V-E.

I THOUGHT THAT ONCE THE WATER WENT DOWN, I'D BE ABLE TO FIND IT...

BUT I'VE TURNED UP NOTHING...

IN THIS ONCE QUIET PLACE, THERE ARE SIGNS OF UNREST.

KLANG KLANG KLANG

THE GUY WHO OWNS THE VALLEY MUST HAVE SEEN ALL THE LANDSCAPING GOING ON HERE AND THOUGHT IT WAS ENCROACHING ON HIS SPACE. NOW HE'S HURRYING TO REDEVELOP TOO AND ASSERT HIS OWNERSHIP.

CLANG CLANG CLANG

THE BOOKS?

I CHECKED THEM ALL OUT.

IF WE EAT DINNER IN GOMORI, DO YOU THINK THE WINDOW WILL BE INSTALLED BY THE TIME WE GET BACK?

PROBABLY...

SIGN: POCHEON MOBILE LIBRARY

COUGH

DAMN IT... THE ROOM'S COVERED IN CONCRETE DUST.

I TOLD THEM TO BE CAREFUL, BUT INSTEAD THEY TOSSED OUT A SLAPDASH EFFORT AND TOOK OFF.

WHIRRRRR   RR

THIS IS JUST TOO MUCH.

WHIRRRR

WHIRR

WHY ARE PEOPLE WHO WORK IN CONSTRUCTION ALL THE SAME?

IF YOU'RE NOT VIGILANTLY WATCHING OVER THEM, THEY'LL TAKE YOUR MONEY, AND THEN THEY'LL SLICE YOUR NOSE OFF TOO. THAT'S THE KIND OF PEOPLE THEY ARE!

HONEY...

WHERE'S YOUR RING?

IT SEEMS LIKE YOU HAVEN'T WORN IT IN AGES.

CHIRP CHIRP CHIRP

VRRRRR

RRRRRRUMBLE BOOM

VWWWRRRRRRAAAAAHHHH

UNGH...

ARE YOU KIDDING ME?! WHAT TIME IS IT?

ARGH

.... ARE YOU AWAKE, HONEY?

NO.

PLEASE FIND YOUR RING.

OH...OF COURSE I WILL.

CLANG CLANG CLANG

IT'S PRETTY REASONABLE FOR HER TO BE ANGRY.

BOOM BOOM BOOM BOOM

BLOOP BLOOP

HELLO THERE.

- - - - HOW DO YOU DO?

IT'S QUITE INTRUSIVE WHEN YOU START CON-STRUCTION AT SEVEN IN THE MORNING.

!

CAN YOU BE MORE CONSIDERATE AND THINK ABOUT THE PEOPLE WHO LIVE HERE?

AH, THAT...SO YOU LIVE IN THAT HOUSE OVER THERE. THE OWNER OVERSTEPPED THEIR PROPERTY LINE WHILE LANDSCAPING THE—

I DON'T CARE ABOUT ANY OF THAT. I'M JUST SAYING THAT THE WAY YOU'RE CONDUCTING YOUR BUSINESS IS MAKING LIFE DIFFICULT FOR US.

· · ·

525

NICE. REEEAL NICE!

MY GOODNESS!

RRREEEAL NICE!!

MR. HONG, WOULD YOU LEND ME A HAND?

OH, OF COURSE!

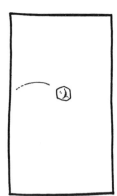

TAK TAK TAK

LET'S GO HOME, OAKIE!

YOU LIL' SCAMP! HOW MANY TIMES DO YOU NEED TO RUN UP AND DOWN THE MOUNTAIN BEFORE YOU'RE HAPPY?

PANT PANT PANT

WOOF WOOF

Winter

HUP!

WIPE WIPE

A WHOLE YEAR'S WORTH OF RUST.

SWEEP SWEEP

LAST YEAR, WHEN WE FIRST STARTED BURNING COAL, WE MISSED THIS STEP AND WASTED A LOT OF EFFORT PUTTING DAMP BRIQUETTES INTO THE STOVE.

BUT THIS WINTER, WE HAVE LEFTOVER COAL FROM LAST YEAR, WHICH WE CAN USE WHILE THE NEWLY ORDERED BRIQUETTES ARE DRYING.

LET'S TRY TO HAVE A GOOD WINTER.

THE THINGS I'VE LEARNED BELONG TO ME. NOW THAT I'VE GOT THE KNOW-HOW, LIGHTING THE BRIQUETTES SHOULD BE EASIER.

WOO HOO— THE STOVE IS BACK!

YOU LIKE IT THAT MUCH?

OF COURSE!

OUR HEATING BILL WITH THE ELECTRIC BOILER WAS MUCH HIGHER THAN EXPECTED.

CHOMP CHOMP

YOU LITTLE PIGS! YOU EAT A WHOLE SACK OF FEED EVERY MONTH, BUT WE'VE YET TO SEE ANY EGGS...

THERE Y'GO!

BOK BOK BOK

CLUCK CLUCK

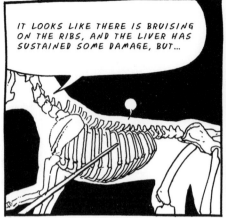

IT LOOKS LIKE THERE IS BRUISING ON THE RIBS, AND THE LIVER HAS SUSTAINED SOME DAMAGE, BUT...

THE MOST URGENT ISSUE AT HAND IS THE JAWBONE SURGERY. UNFORTUNATELY, THE BONE WAS BROKEN AT AN ANGLE, MAKING ANY SURGERY DIFFICULT AND COSTLY, SO...

DOCTOR.

I BROUGHT THIS DOG HOME FROM THE SHELTER TO GIVE IT A SAFE AND HAPPY LIFE.

EVEN IF HE'LL NEVER BE BACK TO NORMAL, PLEASE GIVE HIM THE TREATMENT HE NEEDS TO LIVE WITHOUT TROUBLE.

...

I UNDERSTAND. IF THAT'S THE CASE, RESETTING HIS JAWBONE AND SUTURING HIS FLESH WOUNDS SHOULD BE RELATIVELY SUFFICIENT.

BITING FOOD WITH HIS FRONT TEETH WILL BE DIFFICULT FOR HIM, AND HE WILL DROOL MORE THAN BEFORE, BUT I WILL TREAT HIM AS BEST I CAN SO THAT HE CAN CONTINUE TO LIVE A GOOD LIFE.

THANK YOU, DOCTOR.

534

535

EVEN THAT DESPICABLE IRON STRUCTURE IS COVERED IN A BLANKET OF WHITE SNOW.

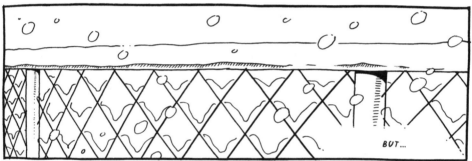

BUT...

WHY CAN'T THAT SAME SNOW COVER THE HATRED SPEWING OUT OF MY HEART?

WHAT KIND OF PERSON WOULD TAKE OAKIE, FRIGHTEN HIM, AND BEAT HIM WITH AN IRON PIPE?

OAKIE MUST HAVE DEFENSIVELY BIT DOWN ALONG THE PIPE AND TRIED TO YANK IT AWAY; ALL IT LEFT BEHIND WAS A BROKEN JAW AND IRON DUST ON THE INSIDE OF HIS MOUTH.

WHAT KIND OF PERSON DOES THAT? ONE THING'S FOR SURE—THEY MUST HAVE BEEN FILLED WITH TREMENDOUS SPITE TO DELIBERATELY HIKE ALL THE WAY UP HERE AND COMMIT THIS ACT.

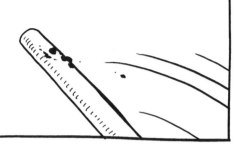

THE VILLAGER WHO PURPOSELY LEFT THEIR TRASH BAGS IN FRONT OF OUR HOUSE LAST SUMMER?

DID SOMEONE IN TOWN HATCH THEIR PLAN ONE OF THOSE TIMES OAKIE ESCAPED AND RAN DOWN THE MOUNTAIN?

MAYBE SOMEONE WHO WAS UNHAPPY THAT I TOOK AWAY THEIR PARKING SPOT TO BUILD THE GARDEN?

THE YOUNG HOODLUMS WHO FREQUENTLY COME UP TO THE VALLEY IN THE MIDDLE OF THE NIGHT TO DRINK?

IF ONLY I COULD CATCH THEM...IF ONLY I KNEW WHO IT WAS...

I DON'T EVEN KNOW WHO I'M IN CONFLICT WITH, WHO THE TARGET OF MY HATRED IS...

BUT THIS CONFLICT AND HATRED HAVE INFECTED MY HEART.

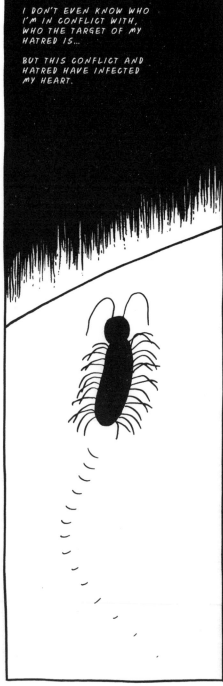

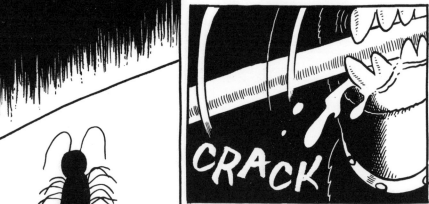

PANT PANT
PANT

ARE WE READING THE NEWS, OR ARCHIVING HISTORY HERE, HM?

TSK

WANNA GO INTO TOWN?

PANT PANT PANT

IF YOU SEE THE PERSON THAT HIT YOU, JUST BARK. I'LL TAKE CARE OF THE REST.

PANT PANT

AFTER THAT DAY, OAKIE NEVER SET FOOT IN THE VILLAGE AGAIN.

WE DON'T HAVE TO IF YOU DON'T WANT TO.

...

WHEN DID THE NEIGHBOR GET HERE?

RING

BRRRING

HELLO?

CLICK

...YES, HELLO, MA'AM.

...

YES, YES.

HA!

SPLISH

BURNING COAL IS THE BEST WAY TO SAVE ON THE HEATING BILL.

AH, IT'S SO WARM!

TSSS

TSSS

HE'S HIKED UP THE MOUNTAIN ALONE AGAIN.

HELLO? I SEE YOU WALKING UP HERE OFTEN THIS TIME OF DAY.

RIGHT UP UNTIL SHE DIED, MY WIFE AND I WOULD HIKE UP THIS MOUNTAIN TOGETHER...

I SEE...

I COULDN'T EVEN SEE WHAT WAS RIGHT IN FRONT OF ME...

IN AUTUMN, YOU WOULDN'T BELIEVE HOW DELIGHTED SHE WAS WHEN I'D COLLECT THE FALLEN CHESTNUTS FROM THIS HUGE TREE...

NOW, I JUST WALK UP HERE BY MYSELF.

...

SCRAPE

DIG

RUMBLE

549

THE OWNER HAS DUG LINES INTO THE EARTH AND PILED ROCKS. THE NEIGHBOR ON THE VALLEY SIDE HAS SECTIONED OFF HIS LAND WITH A CHAIN-LINK FENCE...

CLANG
CLANG CLANG
CLANG

SCRAAAAPE

SCRAPE

APPARENTLY, ANOTHER LANDOWNER
ACROSS THE VALLEY LEVELED PART
OF THE MOUNTAIN IN SECRET TO
WIDEN HIS PROPERTY.

THIS UNSTABLE SITUATION IS JUST...DON'T YOU THINK THIS IS A SIGN THAT WE NEED TO LEAVE NOW?

IF WE STAY HERE IN THE MIDDLE OF THIS LANDOWNER FIGHT, ONLY OUR BACKS WILL EXPLODE.*

*A REFERENCE TO THE KOREAN PROVERB, "IN A WHALE FIGHT, ONLY THE SHRIMP'S BACK EXPLODES."

...YOU ASLEEP?

MM...

· · ·

WHERE DO WE MOVE TO...

HOO

HOO

HOOOO

Spring, And...

TEXT: LAIKA SPEAKS BY SOHMI LEE

IT'S YOUR FIRST BOOK.

. . .

WHAT A FANTASTIC DEBUT.

THE BOOK CAME OUT NICELY, DIDN'T IT?

THIS IS JUST THE BEGINNING, SO ON TO THE NEXT BOOK... LET'S MAKE THE NEXT ONE JUST AS GOOD.

FROM NOW ON, PLEASE ADDRESS ME AS "SOHMI LEE, CHILDREN'S BOOK AUTHOR AND ILLUSTRATOR."

AHEM.

OF COURSE! OF COURSE!

555

WE'VE GRILLED SO MANY CLAMS AND SO MUCH MEAT IN THIS SPOT.

YOU'D THINK WE'D BE SICK OF IT BY NOW.

AHH—

AH

NNNGH, IT TASTES SO GOOD.

NOM NOM

YOU GUYS, COME SIT WITH US.

MEOWWW—

THIS PLACE WAS SO GOOD FOR YOU GUYS...

...

GULP GULP GULP

YOU TOO!

YOU CAME!

YUM YUM

GIMME ANOTHER.

I CAN'T MISS OUT ON THE EATS!

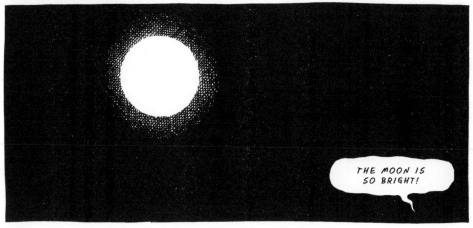

THE MOON IS SO BRIGHT!

IF THERE'S A WAY TO START, THEN THERE'S A WAY TO END—

OUR SEPARATION FROM JUKYEOP MOUNTAIN—

WOBBLE

WOBBLE

SIGNIFIES OUR NEW BEGINNINGS~

SING IT

AHOY

THAT'S RIGHT—

WE'VE LEARNED ALL WE CAN, AND NOW WE ARE LEAVING THE MOUNTAIN—

THE MOON IS AS
BRIGHT AS THE SUN—

AND WE HEAR THE CHORUS
OF EVERY BIRD AND INSECT—

HOW THE WIND BLOWS FROM
BEYOND THE MOUNTAIN—

HOW THE SEEDS WE PLANT
GROW AND GROW AND GROW—

WE EVEN CAME TO
KNOW LONELINESS—

AND SO, ON THIS MOUNTAIN,
WE CAME TO KNOW HOW MUCH
WE RELY ON ONE ANOTHER—

NOW THE IMPORTANT THING IS...

ONCE WE LEAVE THIS MOUNTAIN, WE'LL BE HEADED SOMEWHERE—

OFF TO MEET THAT NEW SOMETHING—

AND IN THAT PLACE, I'LL HAVE MY WORK—

AND YOU'LL HAVE YOURS—

AND WE'LL HAVE OUR LIVES TO KEEP LIVIN'. THAT'S THE TRUTH—

Departure

YOU'RE MOVING?!

WHERE...

WE'RE LOW ON FUNDS, SO WE HAD A HARD TIME FINDING A PLACE, BUT MY WIFE MANAGED TO GET HER PUBLISHER TO LEND US A STUDIO.

THANK GOODNESS. TO BE HONEST... WE'RE LEAVING HERE TOO.

WHAT?!

MY FATHER PASSED AWAY A FEW DAYS AGO. WE BUILT THIS HOUSE FOR HIM TO LIVE IN ONCE HE GOT BETTER, BUT OUR HOUSE IN SEOUL ISN'T SELLING, SO WE'RE RENTING THIS PLACE OUT AND MOVING BACK.

I SEE...

THE SCENERY AROUND HERE WILL PROBABLY CHANGE COMPLETELY, EH?

PERHAPS...

THUMPA THUMPA

GOT MORE LIQUOR?

DA-DUM BOOM

THUMPA THUMPA

WOO!

BOTTOMS UP!

THE OWNERS WERE CONSIDERATE ENOUGH TO LET US STAY THROUGH THE SUMMER.

WE RECLAIMED THE UNUSED GARDEN AND PLANTED NEW CROPS.

WE SWAM BACKSTROKE AT THE SEONNYO POOL.

WE'VE PACKED EVERY-THING, RIGHT?

HOO—
HOO—

YEP!

NOW THAT WE'RE ACTUALLY LEAVING, I DON'T FEEL ANYTHING.

HOO—

HOO—

EVEN THOUGH IT'S OUR LAST NIGHT HERE...

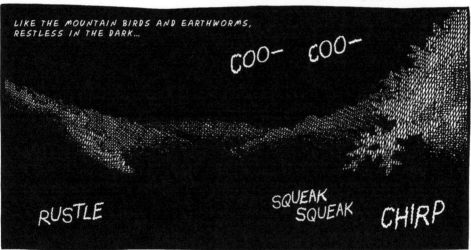

IN 2007, AROUND THE END OF THE
SUMMER, WE LEFT THE MOUNTAIN.

A SHORT, SHORT HISTORY OF A COUPLE—

END.

Afterword
by Hellen Jo

I initially accepted the assignment of translating *Uncomfortably Happily* with some trepidation. Not only would my Korean reading comprehension skills be put to the test (a nightmare scenario for many of us second-generation Korean Americans), but through my reading of Yeon-sik Hong's memoir, I knew I would compare myself to him and come to question my relevance as an artist, as well as the authenticity of my own "Korean-ness." Growing up in the States, I have never felt "Korean enough" nor understood what that meant.

What I learned, however, was that Mr. Hong and I actually have a great deal in common; we are both short-fused, easily distracted procrastinators who let our own panic and dread loom so large in our minds that we wage and lose entire wars within our own heads. We expect a lot of ourselves, and when we fall short of those expectations, we tumble down a deep, dark hole of nihilism regarding our futures and our self-worth. We are complete crap at handling stress.

There were so many instances as I read this book where I would stop, grab my boyfriend, and yell in his face, "IS THIS US?!" I strongly identified with the fatalistic Korean self-loathing and insecure rage, but even the story details seemed to mirror our own lives much too closely for comfort. I had experienced the same stress of dealing with work revisions in my previous life as a storyboard artist, and like Hong, I became adept at avoiding my animation directors, comics publishers, and the editor of this very book. Having just moved into our first home together, my boyfriend and I also experienced the same house worries, yard work distractions, money fears. I would often follow my domestic fears with despair over a wayward career without focus, and like Hong, I felt those same relationship and career insecurities as I watched my partner, a fellow artist, pursue his own career goals and succeed beyond his expectations. I wallowed in self-pitying tantrums of my own professional jealousy, while my boyfriend channeled Hong's own ever-patient wife and endured my despair spirals.

The book was such an eerily exact mirror that at times I was afraid to read it and see more of myself. Hong used this story to explore and resolve the aspects of his own personality that he most detested, and because his character resonated so deeply, it was difficult to see those same flaws reflected back at me. But I appreciated so much that he was able to know himself so completely, and rather than give in to despair, use his new understanding to achieve a more balanced and peaceful existence. It was surreal but reassuring to see in Mr. Hong a kindred spirit, an artist full of insecurity and despair who was ultimately able to lift himself up. Maybe I'm more Korean than I ever knew.

I would like to thank my editor at Drawn & Quarterly, Tracy Hurren, for her infinite well of patience, kindness, and encouragement while working on this book. I would also like to thank Dr. Sahie Kang for her proofreading help and native Korean insights, as well as being a cool mom. Thanks, Omma!

I hope you enjoy this book, and that it brings you the same sense of hope and purpose that it did for me.

Love,
Hellen